T0162297

Where God Comes From

Reflections on Science, Systems and the Sublime

Ira Livingston

Winchester, UK
Washington, USA

First published by Zero Books, 2012
Zero Books is an imprint of John Hunt Publishing Ltd., Laurel House, Station Approach,
Alresford, Hants, SO24 9JH, UK
office1@jhpbooks.net
www.johnhuntpublishing.com
www.zero-books.net

For distributor details and how to order please visit the 'Ordering' section on our website.

Text copyright: Ira Livingston 2011

ISBN: 978 1 78099 400 0

A CIP catalogue record for this book is available from the British Library.

Design: Stuart Davies

Printed in the USA by Edwards Brothers

We operate a distinctive and ethical publishing philosophy in all
areas of our business, from our global network of authors to
production and worldwide distribution.

Where God Comes From

Reflections on Science,
Systems and the Sublime

CONTENTS

Introduction

The Vision of Ezekiel and the Films of Stanley Kubrick

Reflection does not withdraw from the world . . .; it steps back to watch the sparks of transcendence fly up like sparks from a fire; it slackens the intentional threads which attach us to the world and thus brings them to our notice; it alone is consciousness of the world because it reveals the world as strange and paradoxical. (Merleau-Ponty)

I.

Imagine that you and I are on a cross-country road trip, and that we've pulled off the highway somewhere in Montana.

It's late and it's dark, and we're standing, leaning up against the car, watching a distant thunderstorm.

The lightning flashes are the kind that branch out fractally, cloud-to-cloud and cloud-to-ground, more like episodes than single strikes.

Each flash momentarily lights up the gothic sky, the intricate terrain of badlands and canyons laid out in front of us,

and our faces and eyes — before plunging us back again into the big rural darkness.

And imagine that — in an eerie moment of uncertain duration — we become aware that, standing just a few yards in front of us, is *a giant bison*, head bent to the earth, grazing by the roadside

and keeping an eye on us — an eye that gleams with the reflected flashes of lightning. If our vision were good enough,

we would see ourselves reflected in the bison's eye, and the forking lightning in our own reflected eyes.

Some things can only be seen intermittently — only for a moment — even if it is a long moment.

The lightning flash is one instance, and in it, the moment when we first realized another being was there with us.

Neurologists have found that our brains seem to be wired with a kind of detector for the presence of other beings —

and our hair wired to stand up in the moment this brain circuitry is tripped in just the right way.

Even so, if we were so inclined, we might also have experienced this moment as a *religious* one.

The looming, dreadlocked bison — with the nobility of power in repose — does cut a godlike figure!

Or the experience might be cast as an *aesthetic* one, what a generation of college students learned to call an *epiphany*,

using the term aesthetics borrowed from religion (where it refers to *the manifestation of a deity*).

At least for the kinds of people likely to be stopping by the roadside on a cross-country car trip —

modern people, taking a moment out of their goal-directed, machine-enabled and largely bisonless lives —

the experience might well fall somewhere *between* the religious and aesthetic, in the territory sometimes called the *sublime.*

In this case, the sublime flashes in a momentary spark across the chasm between *culture* and *nature* — the chasm we moderns look back across

(but that, on closer examination, turns out to be less singular and more like the intricate terrain of canyons our road straddles).

Of course, sublime moments can be conscripted to shore up the gridded life they might otherwise challenge —

as if we were to pause to text OMG JUST SAW GIANT BISON and then get back on the road. But even so,

this scene — the forking lightning, the maze of canyons, the looping circuits of reflections and awareness among us and the bison —

exhibits all the features of *the architecture of complexity* that is the subject of this book.

And when I say *this scene,* I also include *this very scene,* of this text being written and read, right now,

the scene of metacognition now taking place, in which some trace of the sublime may be found, regardless of whether the scene by the highway really occurred (though I can assure you,

it did).

In starting to look for where the sublimity comes from, you might reflect on the fact that, as you probably know,

lightning is formed by a buildup of electrical charge that, when released, finds multiple paths

(more accurate to say the lightning *is* the multiple paths) again and again to local equilibria.

Curiously, the canyonlands were formed in much the same way, by water meeting resistance and being blocked,

breaking through, finding its way around obstacles, finding multiple paths, some dead ends, others flowing through, again and again —

and you and I and the bison occupy branches and twigs of a similar forking structure called *evolution.*

If branching is differentiation, it also exhibits self-similarity at various scales and across otherwise wildly different phenomena

and these resonances or resemblances continually loop and braid the branches back into a kind of nest, a world, *nested worlds.*

One way of looking at this scene is that you and I are the writer and reader on a road trip, the road is this book,

the lightning flashes are the chapters, and the moment — when we recognize both otherness and kinship —

is what I'm trying to deliver at least intermittently throughout — and, who knows, maybe the bison is a god after all!

This book sets out to anatomize such moments, not to deflate but to sustain them, to prolong them into thought.

II.

Most of the time, an electron bound to an atom sits in an unchanging energy state. To catch one being interesting, you must first throw something at it to provoke it to move, and then snap its picture.

A particle accelerator, like Stanford's Linear Accelerator Center (SLAC), may be among the most extreme examples

of an apparatus for producing insights only sustainable for a moment:

years and years, millions of dollars, teams of massively educated scientists, and massive, mind-bendingly intricate machinery,

all go to create tiny flashes so vanishingly brief they make the blink of an eye seem practically eternal.

SLAC was built on the grounds of the old Palo Alto Stock Farm where, in 1877, Eadweard Muybridge

built a series of cameras and tripwires to resolve the age-old question of whether all four of a horse's hooves

leave the ground at the same time during a gallop. Happily, for the purposes of this book (and for a horse), they do.

Muybridge made a kind of flip-book apparatus to show his photo sequences, a proto-film-projector he called a *zoopraxiscope*.

This book is a kind of zoopraxiscope for airborne moments of cognition that otherwise go by in such a complex flurry

we could doubt that they exist at all.

Imagine that, by some exquisite convulsion, you could jump out of language, out of your own head,

out of the loop between the world and your head and language, but that it took so much torque or spring to do so

that it could only be sustained for a moment before the haze of familiarity settled back on everything like white on rice.

Imagine a poet laboriously crafting a poem. Ordinary language is poetic through-and-through already —

intricately rhythmed and lit by flashes of wordplay and images — but a poem is a more systematically,

more self-consciously sustained performance. Poetry emerges from everyday language and life like a fish jumping out of water.

It requires a mustering of effort and concentration, like the wind-up and release of a spring,

and because it's so heightened, it can only be sustained for a long moment before falling back into the prosaic.

Why do fish jump? To escape predators, from sheer playfulness, or from some ambition to be birds?

(You might notice that all of these are ways of talking about what is otherwise called *evolution*.)

Whatever the combination of reasons, the poem is not just the airborne moment, but the wind-up, the take-off and the splashdown

rolled into one. Poetry is one example, but all systems in relation to their environments are like this,

the rolled-into-oneness being a system's continuous relationship with its environment.

But poetry and language aren't just fish-and-water, system-and-environment. Language is another full-fledged system itself;

a bigger fish. Language itself seems to have jumped or crawled — or at any rate, to have emerged —

from *indexical* communication (as it is sometimes called), which refers to things *by association*, for example,

as a monkey alarm call is triggered by a potential predator and, in turn, triggers responses in fellow monkeys.

One call means *Leopard! Climb up a tree!* and another means *Eagle! Climb down a tree!*,

but survival depends on the call and response remaining tightly tethered to what triggered them, not as in language, where you have — presumably — just read the word *Leopard!* without looking around in terror and climbing a tree!

Symbolic communication sustains reference to the world, but only via a system of elaborate relationships of signs to each other —

an inner ecology of grammar, syntax, and elaborately differentiated sounds and categories.

The emergence of symbolic from indexical communication — the coming-into-its-own of language — is diagrammed beautifully

in anthropologist Terrence Deacon's book *The Symbolic Species: The Co-evolution of Language and the Brain*

as a leap — with a spin — that escapes but stays in orbit over its world, as if a bone, thrown, wheeling, into the air

were somehow to become a spaceship.

Language leaped out of the world, but without ever leaving it (as culture leaped out of nature, but remains in it):

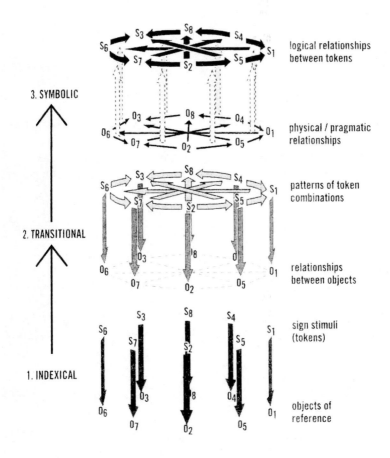

3. SYMBOLIC

logical relationships
between tokens

physical / pragmatic
relationships

2. TRANSITIONAL

patterns of token
combinations

relationships
between objects

1. INDEXICAL

sign stimuli
(tokens)

objects of
reference

Spoken words remain subject to the physics of sound, and ink-on-paper to chemistry, but grammar and syntax

are more like laws-unto-themselves. They can't be reduced to chemistry and physics. Accordingly, we can picture

a system in an environment as a wheel inside a wheel. The big wheel is the laws and constraints it must obey —

or if you prefer the glass-half-full perspective, its *conditions of possibility*.

The little wheel is the leap out of the world, or if you prefer, the leap more deeply into the world:

the system's degrees of freedom — in this case, the extent to which, while never violating the laws of its homeworld,

language dances, but not to the laws of physics —

the way the inner and outer rings of a gyroscope spin independently, but on the same axis.

And the two wheels together are less like an actor and a stage, more like nested systems.

The big wheel is that *by grace of which* the emergent system can come into being (the hands that release the dove),

and the little wheel's *the leap* into uncharted territory, or if you prefer the spiritual version (as Woody Guthrie sang it):

> . . . the little wheel runs by faith
> And the big wheel runs by the grace of God
> And a wheel in a wheel whirling
> Way up in the middle of the air!

III.

Neurohistorian Daniel Lord Smail offers a single explanation for why a whole range of pleasurable experiences —

such as extra-marital sex, masturbation, mind-altering drugs, and individual religious ecstasy —

have had such a history of being stigmatized, criminalized, and psycho-pathologized.

It's because social institutions — like religion and the family — have always sought to retain as much control as possible

over the neurology of pleasure in order to keep our brains wired onto their grid, and to reserve the right

collectively to adjust individual neurochemistry. In this account, modernity has been an ongoing brain rewiring

under the heading of *privatization*, which means not just private *individuals* gaining more of the ability

to adjust their own brain chemistry but also private *corporations* gaining more and more of the prerogative

and the power to do so. This may be just an update of a long-familiar generalization about modernity,

but putting the brain into the picture can transform it (the picture, that is, *and* the brain).

In this account — to pick a contemporary example — digital games are not simply new commodities

capturing a growing share of the leisure/entertainment market (or to put it another way, a huge pop-cultural phenomenon).

What digital games are in the process of capturing is brain wiring and chemistry — and all the money and social relations

wired up with them. The games are parasites on our brain's electro-chemical systems — a collective brain rewiring.

I'm speaking from experience here, since I go into phases of obsessively playing FreeCell, a computer solitaire game,

generally as a work-avoidance strategy. I like to say that work avoidance is a necessary accompaniment to work,

at least when you're a writer. It seems to me that, contrary to expectation, the more work avoidance I do, the more work I also do.

But I say *seems* because, like all addicts, my sense of it can't be trusted!

For one recovering FreeCell addict interviewed in the *New York Times*, Lou Bender (I didn't make that name up),

"the FreeCell habit started as a way to get through boring conference calls at work."

It's easy to recognize the innocuous beginning of the classic addiction narrative.

As it happened, "the feeling the game gave him — *one of getting himself out of a bind* — was irresistible."

The games put you on an *arousal curve* that begins with some kind of tension (however minimal or pleasurable in itself)

and ends with relief. How much tension and how much relief, how easy or quick, or how difficult and long the path from one to the other

are variables that, depending on the context and what works for you, will lead you to prefer one game or activity to another.

The little bind and the little satisfaction of getting out of it can work as defenses against the big bind you can't get out of

and the big satisfaction you can never get. Wracked by shame? Never got unconditional love? Dad and mom never cared?

Never mind: play another game! The narrower explanation is simply that our brains are programmed by evolution

so that the bind-escape mechanism releases pleasurable chemicals: the pigeon pecks the lever and gets a pellet of food.

At worst, we can become addicted to these little doses of power and pleasure, learn to live only for such shallow satisfactions,

and cheat ourselves (or get cheated) out of any chance to attain nobler, more intense, or more sustained rewards.

Content to have climbed to the top of an anthill (one of many *local maxima*), we miss the mountains beyond.

But there is another way of seeing it.

Feelings (like the feeling of tension/frustration and release/satisfaction) can be described as

"the anticipation of a meeting between the subject's body and another's body, real or imaginary."

We get programmed with a range of expectations, a complex *stance* we take in our approach to the world. We learn

to anticipate stimulation, comfort, pleasure, neglect, violence — all arrayed in a more predictable or unpredictable range.

And because of the looping ways our approaches are wired to others' responses and vice versa,

the whole circuitry constitutes a nonlinear structure — a system — of feeling.

Even if the games function as a defense, keeping us stuck, they might serve some *healing* function as well,

rewiring our brains, helping us to anticipate pleasure, orienting us towards finding our way out of binds.

Some experiences one wants to repeat over and over, like opening presents on Christmas morning.

In some sense each is the same as all others of its kind — and totally different. Sex can be like this. Meals. TV. Books.

Even games of computer solitaire. And language is like this: the same few letters and symbols, over and over and over,

the play of sameness and difference — as if writing were repetition, and the writer were the caretaker of a haunted hotel,

typing the same sentence over and over, and rearranging it on the page into a series of different genres.

Wittgenstein made philosophy sound a little like FreeCell when he said that it "unties knots in our thinking;

hence its result must be simple, but its activity must be as complicated as the knots it unties."

The knots, according to Wittgenstein, are the metaphors by

which we think, and which hold our thinking captive.

Untying them does not result in scientific, metaphor-free thought but in facing and embracing a kind of Zen silence

at the core of thought. However, since one of the knots I'm trying to untie here is the sometimes thought-crippling opposition

between the complex and the simple, how could I use the metaphor of untying a knot while rejecting this opposition?

In describing the layout of this book, I might highlight the differences among its sections (this one's a kind of prose poem

in Twitter-length blips, the next a dialogue, then some essays, a bit of literary criticism, and finally a story)

or the big arc these heterogeneous bits make, beginning with beginnings and ending with endings and returns,

but at the moment I prefer to represent the arc and the differences as subordinated to *repetition*,

a FreeCell game played over and over. Having already set aside the metaphor of untying a knot,

let me say instead that each game is a stitch in an embroidery, each stitch a little metacognitive leap

that gets looped back into the fabric of thought and feeling. Or if you prefer the spiritual version, it's a kind of rosary:

> The band in heaven, they play my favorite song
> Play it once again, play it all night long (David Byrne)

IV.

In the late eighteenth century in Europe there was a sustained explosion, an ongoing *tsunami* of the written word —

of books, newspapers, magazines, private letters, broadsheets, posters: all of what is now called *print culture*.

Wordsworth complained, in 1799, about the new thirst for stimulation that "the rapid communication of intelligence hourly gratifies."

(Apparently he was referring to newspapers, but there were also two mail deliveries per day in London at that time.)

He denounced "frantic novels" and the "deluges of idle and extravagant stories in verse," fearing

that all this might "blunt the discriminating powers of the mind" and "reduce it to a state of almost savage torpor."

The complaint about new media — that it is making us stupid — has been repeated so many times, in much the same terms

about television, the internet, electronic games, and so on, that one could lose sight of something odd here:

Wordsworth was complaining about *literacy*, about reading and writing making people stupid.

Print culture was a type of cyberspace — that is, a virtual realm removed from but highly connected to the world —

a place that increasingly came to mediate people's relationships with themselves and others, a collective brain rewiring.

But language itself — signed or spoken or however it got started — was just such a place as well —

and also a parasite with which our brains have co-evolved.

Do new media make us dumber or more intelligent? Do they free us, or exert ever more insidious control?

Are we stuck with the same thing over and over and over, or are we embarked on an evolutionary series

of radical transformations? And what does it mean that we can entertain such profound uncertainty

about the path we're on and where we're going?

V.

Everywhere I walk, people are on cellphones. This looks like what used to be called *communication*,

but for whatever combination of reasons, cellphones seem to be particularly good for *venting* — or at least,

it seems to me that venting occupies a much greater percentage of the cellphone conversations

than the person-to-person conversations I pass on the street. I can only theorize that the cellphone

is another kind of bind/release mechanism. Apparently, whenever you get frustrated and angry,

you can *get a witness* instantly and get some relief (which is why it isn't exactly two-way communication).

But does venting make people *less* frustrated and angry or, by reinforcing the emotional stance of venting, more?

Is the demand that others adopt the role of witnesses to how put-upon we are part of *the structure of feeling*

one might expect in a declining imperial nation: the tone of indignation and affronted privilege?

I was walking in Brooklyn (where I live) and passed several people walking while talking and texting on phones.

I suddenly felt like there had been some kind of apocalypse, like everyone had been raptured

into the *cellphonosphere*, and I was the only one left in public, bodily social space.

I could have said the others were still physically walking around but had been turned into social zombies, not really there.

But it wasn't that kind of movie for me. It felt good; I was *left behind*! And for now, the world was all mine.

This will only make finding other survivors all the sweeter.

VI.

By most accounts, there was a tipping point for Western modernity around 1800 —

what amounted to a reorganization of the whole landscape of human activity and experience.

This included the naming of *aesthetics* as a distinct sphere of human experience and as an object of study,

and along with it, art and literature as categorically distinct from other discourses and experiences.

Art had been overwhelmingly and literally part of religion. It wasn't just plastered inseparably onto cathedral walls,

it *was* the walls. But from the Renaissance onward, art got increasingly pried away from the walls

and made into a portable commodity (a painting on canvas, you could say, is more like a big dollar bill than it is like a cathedral).

This is why Samuel Taylor Coleridge considered artists and other cultural producers to be lay priests (*clerisy* was his word),

and early 20th-century critic T. E. Hulme defined Romanticism as "spilt religion."

This must also be why the Romantics liked the myth of Prometheus, the hero/antihero who stole fire from the gods.

Keeping the neurohistorical perspective in mind, we could say that the stolen fire was the actual fire in the brain,

the neurochemical and electrical lightning flashes transferred from religious to aesthetic experience.

The privatization of aesthetic experience was also a way of containing its potential for proliferating meaning,

or as French philosopher Michel Foucault put it, "the great danger with which fiction threatens the world" (reminding us, that *privacy* used to be a negative word — associated with exclusion — with privation and deprivation).

The problem was not that religion was spilled, but in how it was sopped up.

Not just experience but ideas were also subject to widespread systematicization

into distinct discourses and disciplines (such as *science* and *literature*, two categories that may now seem timeless

but, in fact, only began to be used in their modern sense in the nineteenth century).

Can art, religion, and ideas be stolen again?

Are we in the middle of an ongoing reorganization of human experience and thought that will leave the landscape as changed,

changed utterly, as modernity transformed Europe two hundred years ago?

I think so, but it is not my purpose here to try to stand back in order to survey the landscape, as one must do

in order to take the metadisciplinary view or to make historical claims (as I was trained to do, and as I've done in previous books).

You can stay on your anthill only so long. If you want to have any hope of reaching the mountains beyond,

you have to go down, into the valleys where you lose your path and perspective, and keep on walking.

This book explores how the sublime and miraculous can be found in a whole range of processes —

from chemistry and biology to language and literature and social interactions —

and how they loop back on themselves to form complex systems and stitch themselves and their environments together.

The essays that follow — on topics ranging from music to road trips and chaos theory — explore mystical experience

as what happens when consciousness discovers its family resemblances with other recursive processes.

The process has been for me, and I hope will be for you, a cognitive journey of many detours,

in which getting stuck turns out to be the way to make a breakthrough, and getting lost the way to find something new.

Chapter One

Miracles and Signs

I. Recognition to Infinity

The seed that grew into this book was planted in 2007, when I decided to look up Professor Lee, a friend of my father's and of my family since I was a child. When I was in college — late in the last millennium — I used to have long, free-ranging talks with him. He introduced me to systems theory, which turned out to be important to my own research, though I didn't follow him into the sciences.

I hadn't seen him in twenty years. As it turned out, he had just moved into an old folks home in the Bronx, a subway ride away from where I live in Brooklyn, so I went to visit him.

At seventy-five, he still looked exactly as he had when I was a child and tagged along on hikes with him and my father. On one of these hikes, he took the photo below of me and my sister and father, and our dog. Not to sound too melancholic, but all the fields and trees in the photo are long gone, leveled by a kind of nuclear blast of suburbanization that left only condo developments, strip malls and asphalt in its wake. My father is long dead. And the little dog, too!

The first time I visited the Professor in the Bronx we redis-covered an old rapport that had improved with age, as if, without us even checking in on it for all those years, it had just been maturing in the barrel the whole time. On a whim, I asked him to come with me on a road trip to Minneapolis, our old home town, and he agreed right away.

You could write a book about it, he said. I'll be the wise old professor. People love that shit.

I knew he was thinking of that book, a huge bestseller, in which a guy starts visiting his old professor, who's dying of some horrible disease.

We started playing with the idea. I said that he'd have to sign an agreement whereby every word that came out of his mouth during the trip would be my property. He said okay, but I'd have to omit or disguise any and all personal details of his life — he was dead serious about this — and that I'd have to refer to him only as *Professor Lee* — which, by the way, is not his name. He suggested that the book be called *Roadtrip with Professor Lee*. I protested, only half-jokingly, that the lack of a fully fleshed-out character would hurt book sales, and besides, people would think Lee was just an alter ego of mine, especially since I'm also a professor, and since the Chinese version of my surname also happens to be *Li*. That ambiguity was just perfect as far as he was concerned. You can't write about *me*, he said, but you can still write about whatever *ideas* we talk about.

Then something uncanny happened. He started to smile, and something about the smile made me realize what must have just occurred to him: that I could write as much as I liked about our arrangement (as I am doing now), and the Professor Lee character would *still* seem like an invented alter ego — a metaphor for the plurality of the individual writer. And *he saw* that I had seen what he was thinking. And *I saw that he saw it*, and (I have no doubt) he saw me seeing him see me see him, and so on. Later he would refer to this kind of moment — using his

characteristic mix of systems theory and existential theology —
as *recognition to infinity*. Though it felt like psychic communication to me at the time, it's really a very common experience, just
a little feedback loop. We both knew what had happened — or at
least, I thought at the time that I did, and I didn't find out until
much later that I was almost completely wrong. For the moment,
there was no need to talk about it.

He said the Professor Lee character should be whimsical and
philosophical in the face of some terminal illness. We joked about
what illness to give him, not knowing that he'd be dead for real
in a little less than a year. Well, I didn't know, anyway — I can't
say for sure if he did at that point. In any case, I promised him I
wouldn't write about any of the details.

We never made the trip, but I saw him many times in the
months that followed my initial visit, and this book is partly the
record of how those conversations rewired my brain. I've started
off by trying to reconstruct one of our conversations, constrained
as I am by the Professor's injunction to keep him out of it (and by
my own tendency to make dialogue sound like academic prose,
which admission I'm placing here in parentheses to soften it a bit,
and also — as discreetly as possible — to ask for your indul-
gence). Accordingly, the rest of this chapter is an amalgam of our
early conversations about miracles and signs, in which many of
the ideas explored in subsequent chapters are introduced.

The chapters that follow are more typical linked essays,
though in both form and content, I hope I have managed to keep
some of what I found most enjoyable about our conversations —
namely, the way detours and tangents get woven together to
constitute the fabric of ideas explored here.

I've also included, toward the end the book, a short account of
the road trip Professor Lee and I had planned, and which —
although I had to make it alone — seemed somehow to have been
scripted by him.

One of the Professor's favorite references, psychoanalyst D. W.

Winnicot, liked to say that we simultaneously both *find* and *invent* the world. For the Professor, this was why certain signs and people — that we seem merely to have stumbled upon — seem to have been sent to us as revelations, soul mates, mythic guides and guardian angels. But rather than deflating what had seemed miraculous, the explanation points the way to what the Professor had no qualms in calling *a real miracle* — in the way that systems relate to their environments and meaning is propagated in the universe. He saw no contradiction between hardnosed scientific study and mystical awe; in fact, he was one of those who regarded the former as a path to the latter, and vice versa.

II. The Gravity Suspension Miracle

Perhaps kindling in the amygdala causes every external event and internal belief to acquire deep significance for the patient, so there is an enormous proliferation of spuriously self-relevant beliefs and memories in his brain. (V.S. Ramachandran)

Theoretical physics . . . is fiction constrained by fact, fiction that must lift itself in the air together with the hard facts on which it is based. It is like the castle in René Magritte's famous painting — a massive rock hovering over the sea that ought to collapse but is in fact suspended by the mysterious power of its internal consistency. (Giovanni Vignale)

Professor Lee was a religious anarchist: he thought that everybody should start their own religions. Shortly after I started visiting him in the Bronx, he asked me if I had ever experienced any miracles around which to build a religion of my own. I tried to sidestep the question, but he pestered me to tell him anything that might serve the purpose, no matter how trivial.

The first thing that popped into my head was my longstanding notion that, once when I was a child, I had jumped up into the air and stayed up longer than the laws of physics allow. I don't know how old I was, maybe seven or eight. You'd think something like this would be pretty common for a kid of that age, but for some reason this one had struck me — and stuck with me.

Then, like an oyster building a pearl around a grain of sand, I began to secrete so many layers of ruminations around the event that it started to seem impossible to determine — or just flat-out impossible — that there could have been anything there in the first place. Still, at some level, beyond belief or disbelief, something like a bodily memory of the experience persisted.

Professor Lee laughed. It reminded him of the story of an old Irish peasant woman who entertained the poet W. B. Yeats with accounts of the fairies — the "little people." As Yeats was taking his leave, he asked her whether she herself believed in the fairies, and she dismissively assured him that she did not. As he was walking away, though, she called after him, "but they're there, Mr. Yeats, they're there!"

What I came to believe — I told the Professor — was that I had felt something like an instant of zero gravity at the top of my jump. I assume this must be related to the feeling in the pit of your stomach in an elevator or a roller coaster, but I've never checked with a physicist or a physiologist. The sensation had been real enough, and it may even have involved remarkable hypersensitivity, but the laws of physics remained intact.

Professor Lee liked the story. Well, he said, at bottom it's not a story at all, since the miraculous part of it, the heart of it, is just a single instant. The only story is the *cover story* secreted *around* that instant. In fact, the whole story is like what psychoanalysis calls a *screen memory* wrapped around a primal scene too miraculous, too submerged and too constitutive of your own thought process for you to be able to think it: the emergence of language

26

in your brain.

(You may recognize here the origin of my account, in the introduction to this book, of the emergence of language as a physics-defying leap, though I would have to be struck with it many more times before I finally began to get it.)

He went on to point out the stark contrast between, on one hand, the fleeting mid-jump instant of gravitylessness, and on the other, my subsequent ruminations, which I had compared to the slow secretions of that sedentary and most gravity-bound creature, the oyster.

This contrast between bodily motion and cognitive wheel-spinning made me think of an aphorism of William Blake, and since the Professor had Yeatsed me, I Blaked him back:

> The Emmet's Inch & Eagle's Mile
> Make Lame Philosophy to smile.

The emmet (or as we now call it, the *ant*) and the eagle live in radically different worlds, unknown to each other. The tiny, industrious ant troops alongside hundreds of its fellows, all feeling their way along, completely invisible to the noble eagle, who sweeps across vast terrains, the solitary predator. Lame philosophy smiles at this situation, *ruefully*, because it cannot move at all, neither in inches nor miles, only sit back and contemplate. But philosophy's smile is also *smug* — or transcendental, if you prefer — since philosophy is the only one who can see both of these creatures who cannot see each other — and more than this, the only one with the perspective to see that each creature — *including itself* — is radically limited to its own distinct world. In other words, Blake's little couplet manages to posit three worlds, each with its own kind of creature, each with its own powers and handicaps — or rather, *four*, since who or what is it that describes the first three? The obvious — and Blakean — answer is that *the fourth is the poet.*

Professor Lee remarked that the words *emmet* and *eagle* each have five letters, while *philosophy* — which encompasses both perspectives — has ten. And that the defining measures or markers of each world — *inch*, *mile*, and *lame* — are all four-letter words — to which we might as well add *poem*. And that these curious alignments of signifiers with signifieds are how you know that the poet (not the philosopher) is the one who made it — it's the signature of the poet.

This was clever, but I didn't know what to say. I shrugged my shoulders.

Continuing in a Blakean vein (or so it seemed to me), he observed that a traditional Christian reading of my leap might be that it was an allegory of the soul being given a taste of freedom from its bodily prison — a kind of glimpse of heaven — before being pulled back down to earth again. But, he said, in your case the bodily experience was the miracle, and the immaterial part — the thoughts that clustered around the bodily experience — were what bound you back down to earth.

This (I interjected) was just what Blake meant when he said that "Energy is the only life and is from the Body," in conjunction with his assertion that "Man has no Body distinct from his Soul for that call'd Body is a portion of Soul discern'd by the five senses, the chief inlets of Soul in this Age."

No doubt, Professor Lee remarked, even if what struck you was at first just a twinge in the pit of your stomach, and even if your ruminations magnified it and miraculized it and then tried to neutralize it after the fact, it really did become something you cherished, a spark you carried, a talisman. As a trace of the emergence of language, the moment also records the estab-lishment of a polarity between the miraculous and the mundane. Maybe this unstable polarity that you sustain — or that sustains you — is the systole and diastole of a kind of a beating heart, a motor producing movement and electricity along the axis of the polarity.

All this seemed profound. But halfway through the Professor's rhapsodizing, I had already started thinking of another bodily miracle, which I hastened to relate.

III. The Perfect-Fitting-Clothes Miracle

I remembered a day when I was in graduate school, probably more like half an hour one afternoon, when my clothes seemed to fit me perfectly. I was falling in love, and, appropriately, it was spring, but it's hard to know for sure since it was California, and it really could have been any time of year. I was walking down a wide path with the library on one side and the main quadrangle on the other. In particular, I remember the way my shirt hung from my shoulders and how my clothes moved with me as I walked.

Professor Lee laughed. *That* was it? You must be the world's biggest rationalist for something so small to qualify as a miracle! Doesn't your shirt always hang from your shoulders and your clothes always move with you? Otherwise you'd always be walking out of them, finding yourself naked and having to turn back and pick them up.

I ignored him. Later (I said) it occurred to me, maybe this is how happy people experience their clothes *every day*. But here's the paradox: if they experienced this all the time, how could it feel miraculous to them? Then again, if their chronic happiness levels are higher than mine, maybe their acute happiness episodes are that much more intense as well. Maybe if *they* had a perfect-clothes-fitting day they'd be writhing around on the ground in ecstasy with their eyes rolled back in their heads.

The Professor laughed at my speaking about happiness as a disease and happy people using the word *they*.

It reminded me that I had once told a therapist about another experience of extreme well-being. Of course, I had said, I realize that you can't feel that way *all* the time. What he said was: "*Why not?*" Years of therapy condensed into that two-word challenge:

why not? Maybe these experiences — the perfectly-fitting clothes and the gravity suspension — mark the places where the miraculous joy that could suffuse my life, but which I am afraid would shatter me, glimmers for an instant through a chink in my armor.

I object to your use of the word *chink*, said the Professor. But if you think of what it would mean to have your clothes fit like that every day, you can understand what it must feel like to be *saved*, the Professor said. It's like having lots of money in the bank.

Of course I had to ask: what would *you* know about that?

He let that go by. Every day (he continued) you've got that twinkle in your eye, even when things go wrong, way wrong. Maybe you're even in the back of an ambulance choking on your own blood, your whole sorry life reeling out before your eyes, but somewhere in your mind, it's all trumped by years of the fact that — to hell with it! —- you've still got the money, or the perfectly-fitting clothes. Never mind that they can't save you in the sense of actually preventing you from dying — even Jesus doesn't do that. It's just that they somehow redeem everything else: *O Death, where is thy sting?*

This reminded me of how I sometimes feel about photography: no matter how bad a time I'm having, I feel that it is somehow redeemed by taking photographs. I'll save most of the photos I take, but generally I don't look at them much. It's all about taking the photos, not about using them later as aesthetic objects, spurs to memory, or whatever.

Professor Lee laughed. Notice, he said, that there is a kind of doubling and a looping back: you're having a bad time but you can simultaneously stand back from it to take the photo. This is like being a writer, like using language in the first place, where the act of representation distances the otherwise shattering immediacy of experience, or at least displaces it a bit by reinserting back into the world a representation of the world. This is why you tell a whimpering child to *use your words*. And it can become part of a worldview, a stance in which you understand your life and your experiences as a kind of experiment, whether in a more scientific sense (as an opportunity for extracting knowledge or self-knowledge) or in a more religious sense (as if you were being tried or tested).

Language and thought (the Professor said) — like money in the bank, like a photograph — hang on the world like the clothes hang on your body.

As Professor Lee was talking, I was thinking about how growing up in the tortured melodrama of my own family had spurred me to be an intellectual, and I felt again (as I sometimes do) a surge of gratitude to those otherwise tragic and self-involved characters, my parents. The gratitude came in the form of a pop-song lyric (with apologies to Christina Aguilera): *thanks for making me — a writer*.

The Professor said something disparaging about my mother (whom he had never liked), and then he made a stupid joke about yogurt sauce (that is, *raita*), and then he started off on a tangent about making lemonade from lemons, and the so-called "miracle berries," which make everything sour taste sweet, and all this made me think of another miraculous experience.

IV. The Fried Noodles Miracle

In 1992, during my second year as an Assistant Professor, the executive committee of my department voted not to renew my contract. This was one incident in years of battles with the ruling conservatives (not just at my university, but in the humanities generally) during the period that came to be known as the Culture Wars. The Dean would eventually override the committee's vote, but at that moment it fell on me like a ton of bricks — partly because, back in those days, I still believed that, in spite of the depth of my differences with the conservatives, they would give me a fair hearing.

Professor Lee laughed. You thought you had what is sometimes called *a white man's chance*, he said.

Anyway, the wind was knocked out of me. I called Iona. We had only been together a few months and were still in the first flush of love. She invited me to come over for dinner, and she made stir-fried noodles — *lo mein* — with pork and lots of chiles. These noodles were so good that eating them was actually life-changing. It was as if there were two roads: one of bitterness and the other of joy, and in the process of eating them, I was knocked off my horse and put on the right path — a genuine conversion experience.

Well, said the Professor, upon sober consideration one could say that it wasn't just the noodles but the whole situation — your experience of Iona's love and care, and the pleasure of eating, along with your simply being ready to stop sulking and move on, and needing only the slightest encouragement — that enabled you to put your toxic colleagues — or even your whole academic career — back into perspective.

Or one could speculate that the neurological effect of the chiles — yes, it's been scientifically proven! — triggered a cascade of well-being in your brain, probably related to the temporal-lobe stimulation known to be associated with religious experience.

But even if you accept all these explanations — and I do, actually — the fact remains that the message was actually *delivered* by the noodles — call it the annunciation — and thus the power to deliver this message really was *in* the noodles — call it transubstantiation, just as Catholics believe the wafer actually becomes the body of Christ — or as Jews and Chinese people believe, Food Is Love. Even so, a lesser cook might not have been able to conjure up such messianic *lo mein*!

This seemed right to me. I reminded Professor Lee that a woman in Florida had found the face of the Virgin Mary on a grilled cheese sandwich (which later sold for big money on Ebay).

The miracle, said the Professor, is the fit between the key and the lock. In fact, though, the key and the lock were actually manufactured to fit together.

This enigmatic statement started him off on a long disquisition on systems theory: he was using the lock and key to represent a system and its environment, but it was hard to tell which was which. Since I had already been reminded of another miracle, I interrupted him.

V. The Miracle of the Materialized Key

I told the story of how my friend Josie had called me, and after we had chatted for a while, she admitted that she was just trying to kill time while locked out of her apartment and waiting on the stoop for her boyfriend David to show up, in about an hour. I said it was too bad that the key wasn't still under the flowerpot, where I had left it — as instructed — when I had taken care of their cats more than a month earlier. She had forgotten about this — and who knows, maybe David had forgotten about too. She lifted up the flowerpot — and yes! There was the key!

To be able to solve a friend's problem out of the blue, *remotely*, as if I had made the key materialize out of thin air, miles away, just when it was needed, was supremely satisfying.

Professor Lee laughed. Knowing you even as little as I do, he said, I can see how this speaks to your own messianic dream of yourself, and thus why it would feel like a miracle. In your writing, you hope to be able to provide to your readers — from afar, as it were, since all writers work from afar — even those readers who have come to you (as your friend did) merely to spend an idle hour — the key to resolve their most pressing problems.

What you really did was enable the conversion of a key piece of *information* into a physical key. The revelatory part of this is the miraculous nature of information, a kind of holy ghost, mediating between the immaterial and the material worlds, crossing temporal and spatial distance, connecting brains and bodies. Or if you're a monist, you could just say that everything is a seamless web of information, meaning and materiality together.

We started talking about semiotics, the study of signs. The Professor quickly brought the conversation around to the religious sense of signs, and he asked me to tell him about any such signs I had experienced.

VI. The Mockingbird Sign

I immediately thought of my last day of teaching at Stony Brook University. At the end of the day, I climbed the stairs to the top of the three-level parking lot that overlooks the Humanities Building where my office was.

Walking out of the stairwell, I remembered also having parked there the first day I arrived at Stony Brook, seventeen years earlier. I remembered walking over to the parapet wall, looking down at the shabby two-story building, and being surprised by the gloom-and-doom feeling washing over me, overwhelmed by the sense that I would live out the remainder of my life *here*, and experiencing it not just as a feeling but as the actual future years pressing down on me.

But on this last day, as I walked over to my car, I noticed a bird —a mockingbird, I'm pretty sure — perched on the roof of the stairwell. It was facing the Humanities Building and repeatedly leaping up a couple of feet in the air, fluttering its wings to stay aloft for a moment — an impressive show of bluster — and then settling back on the roof, all the while singing furiously, running through a little medley of songs, rather like a somewhat more melodic car alarm.

Professor Lee laughed. It's a poignant little story, he said, but you don't need a theologian to get to the bottom of it — you need an ornithologist!

I ignored him. Anyway, I said, what occurred to me at the moment was that — as Bob Dylan once said — *I'm just like that bird*, blustering, hopping about, puffing myself up, and running through my little repertoire of assertions and complaints. It seemed that the universe had placed the bird there as if to say to me: little creature, behold yourself! One who plays out his role intensely — who struts and frets his hour upon the stage — but with no perspective, no sense of the cosmic and comic insignificance of his own performance. But it was as if the mirror was being held up not to shame me, but lovingly, indulgently. The bird was not pathetic but sprightly and attractive, a kind of pugnacious cartoon character.

And then, as I was telling Professor Lee about the bird, it occurred to me that I really did have a little repertoire of songs. I had theme music for leaving Stony Brook: Bob Dylan's "I ain't gonna work on Maggie's farm no more." And I had had a song for my tenure battle there: the old Chuck Berry song "You Can't Catch Me." And a starting-again song when I left Stony Brook and took a job at Pratt Institute: Lou Reed's "Beginning of a Great Adventure." Once, in fact, when one of my old graduate students contacted me, struggling to decide whether to quit his job and take a position at a different college, I hit upon this piece of advice: if you find the right theme song, clarity will follow!

That's perfect! the Professor shouted. We'll call our book *Finding Your Theme Music*! And when I pressed him for a subtitle, he came up with *An Infallible Guide to Life's Most Difficult Decisions*.

In fact, Professor Lee said, it seems that music works by finding — or actually by manufacturing — a point of alignment between your thoughts and your feelings, or between the two sides of your brain, or your consciousness and subconsciousness and meta-consciousness, or however you want to put it. It harmonizes them, like a kind of chiropractic adjustment. But it's not just the neurological activities in your brain: it's also a question of orchestrating them with the situation you're in — or to put it in terms of systems theory, it's the way the system/environment dynamics are looped and re-inserted back into the system itself.

And by the way, he said, speaking of loops, notice the strange but unmistakable echo of your childhood leap in the little leaping bird, who — because he's fluttering his wings — really does defy gravity for a moment. Maybe this is also you coming to terms with your own characteristic *defiance*, which I suspect has always been both a necessary asset and a liability.

I was amazed that I hadn't noticed this! And although I was the one who balked at Professor Lee's term *miracle*, I now had to protest that, though his explanation was compelling, he had sidestepped what seemed to be miraculous. How was it that the bird was there at just that place where I'd had my doom-and-gloom moment years earlier, and just at the very moment of my departure?

Well, said the Professor, you could put this in terms of systems theory, but the telegraphed version is that God watches over you, and, at key moments, lets you see yourself mirrored in His loving eyes.

I grimaced. You make Him sound like some gigantic predatory spider!

That's the kind of snarky response one would expect from an intellectual, said the Professor. But at least calling it God acknowledges something miraculous in the moment, something sublime about how systems are embedded in their environments that must always exceed the grasp of the systems themselves. Unfortunately, naming it God can also be used to eclipse what is really miraculous; namely, the complex dynamics of the moment.

Of course, the moment might have been just as cosmically significant if, instead of seeing the bird, you had gotten into your car and seen a ladybug crawling on your rearview mirror, or turned on the radio and heard some particular song, or looked up and saw a flying flock of geese in the shape of the Chinese character for *humanity*. (I told the Professor I had seen that movie, too: Chen Kaige's *Life on a String*.)

This (the Professor continued) is the same reason that horoscopes seem to work: because our brains are so good at making connections, so good at pattern recognition and interpretation, at finding meaning and making it. Interpretation is an elegant adapter to make a square peg fit in a round hole. But this doesn't debunk the meaning or the miracle of signs: it *is* the miracle! And notice that that it's also just the function I claimed for music; to align and orchestrate.

I thought of the Flying Karamazov Brothers, a comedy team that juggles items brought to the stage by audience members. At one performance I saw years before, I remember them juggling together a little cast-iron anvil and some ping-pong balls — an amazing trick of coordination. The Professor liked this image. Any system (he said) is an anvil-and-ping-pong-ball juggling act, a swirling vortex of the heterogeneous stuff it both finds and invents, appropriated into its own components — a little spiral-armed galaxy. That's why I like to say that the name of every system is *Eddy*.

This was one of those moments when I realized that the Professor really had read my books, since he had stolen the idea of system-as-juggling from me — at least I'm pretty sure he had. But I was flattered and felt no need for any acknowledgement.

I admitted that the mockingbird sign was wide open to interpretation. But I thought of another sign involving an uncanny coincidence I didn't think the Professor would be able to explain so easily.

VII. The Jellyfish Sign

I serve on a committee with a close friend of mine, and during one difficult meeting where he and I were on opposite sides of an issue, he made what I felt was an anti-semitic remark, which seemed like it may as well have been calculated to manipulate the ethnic dynamics of the group and secure the non-Jews on his side (which is, in fact, exactly what happened). I was hurt and angry but managed mostly to keep my cool. After the meeting, I couldn't stop obsessing about it. I didn't know if it was calculated or inadvertent, or which was worse, or whether I had misread or magnified whatever move he had been making. But I knew there had been *something* there, some hostility on his part.

The next day I drove out to Long Island, and Iona and I went to the beach. I decided to swim out to where the waves were just breaking over a rock that remained invisible just below the surface, quite a distance out — probably a large, erratic boulder resting on the otherwise flat and sandy bottom. As you may know, Long Island is a terminal moraine — basically a stretched-out pile of sand studded with the occasional boulder, all pushed there by a glacier and left when the glacier receded.

Anyway, as I swam out and began to approach the waves breaking over the rock, I felt something brush against my arm and legs. My body immediately went into startle-response mode, a moment of panic, but I told myself it must have been either seaweed or just a little moving eddy created by my swimming — probably the latter, since it felt strangely soft. Even so, I turned around and started swimming back to shore, silently nagging myself for not pressing on. But then my arm and legs began first to tingle and then to sting, as if I had walked through nettles, and though I tried to tell myself it was probably because the water was cold, or somehow I wasn't breathing properly and getting enough oxygen, the sensation kept getting worse and worse. Close to shore, I barely managed to avoid swimming into a jellyfish floating just below the surface of the water, and I realized that one of these creatures must have stung me. I was afraid Iona wouldn't believe me, since she thinks I'm hypersensitive about things like this. There wasn't even any real mark on my skin, just some vague redness, though the prickling pain continued to intensify before leveling off. It subsided after about an hour.

Much later I realized that my anxiety about Iona had been

largely a projection: after all, *I* was the one who didn't believe me! My original cognitive response to the sensation had been doggedly to try to explain it away — though my body made another decision — and I couldn't quite shake my own dismissiveness, even after I had actually seen the jellyfish and felt the pain.

Strange to say — especially if we are such clever, interpretive creatures as you suggest, Professor — that it wasn't until a couple days later, when I was driving back to Brooklyn, that it struck me: the jellyfish sting had been an uncanny analogue of my friend's remark, and in both cases, even as the stinging got worse and worse before subsiding, even though I knew that *something* had happened, I couldn't tell how much it had been magnified by my own hypersensitivity.

So how do you explain this uncanny alignment between the sting and the stinging remark? In fact my friend had never made any such remark before, and I had never in my life been stung by a jellyfish, and neither of these things has ever happened again, so it's not like there could have been some statistical probability behind it.

First of all, said Professor Lee, there's nothing religious about this sign, at least as you've presented it — it's hard to say even if there's any particular message you feel was being delivered to you. In any case, I'm happy to grant the parallel between the two stings, but I'm more struck by two other parallels it seems you haven't noticed. The first is between the rock over which the waves were breaking — something out-of-place and invisible just below the surface but which can be inferred from the breaking waves — and the two jellyfish, the first that stung you but you never saw, and the second you saw, also just below the surface of the water, that enabled you to infer the first one. And notice that in both cases these are things that you approach but veer away from at the last moment. It's hard not to think that these represent possibly dangerous things just barely submerged *in your own mind.*

I had to admit that this gave me a chill.

But (I protested) I wasn't *dreaming* — all this actually happened! How could things I encounter in the actual world represent the contents of my own mind? That really would be a miracle!

Well, said the Professor, first of all, the little flash of fear that you felt again just now was an entirely appropriate feeling. You were touching what must be one of the keystones of your personality, upon which the whole vaulted and buttressed structure depends! Good thing our brains are wired to feel something intense upon approaching that place.

But in answer to your question: as you well know, we selectively notice things and are selectively attracted to them and selectively fixate on them or fear them. For example, out of all the things one might do at a beach, you were moved to swim out to the rock. And out of all the possible responses to being stung by a jellyfish or a friend's remark, yours — which was again, as it had been with your childhood leap, to spin a cognitive cocoon around it — was not something written into it already but what you brought to it yourself.

So in this sense anyway, he continued, we live in worlds that are largely of our own making. And it's not just that we are selective in what we *notice* or how we *feel*. The selectivity *makes us what we are*: who we are shapes our choices, and our choices loop back to shape who we are. This is actually the paradigm of natural selection, though you have to factor out the simplistic notion of choice. Often these nonlinear, looping interactions simply reinforce and stabilize us and confirm our worldviews, but the point of reinsertion is also the point of vulnerability and potential transformation, so in a very real sense, our identities are at stake at every turn, subject to being reiterated or changed. This is what we approach in mystical experience.

So (I asked), what does my story mean about me, Dr. Freud?

Well, he said, even if I could tell you, you couldn't grasp what it means — not and remain yourself. It's a fact of system architecture. Everything built of information and meaning — like a self — has a blind spot where it is joined to itself and to the world. To confront your own organizing principles — or rather the contradictions around which your system is organized — would either bring the system down or compel it to reorganize with the addition of new meta-levels.

To put it another way, you couldn't just take yourself apart and put yourself back together in a new configuration. At some point you'd be laying disassembled and quivering on a table and thinking: Shit! Now what do I do? And hoping somebody might come along to reassemble you.

Or to put it another way, if you could see God, not just a glimpse but full on, wouldn't it shatter you, instantly evaporate your ego and your intellect? If you could come face to face with God and survive, how could that be God? So if you think about the one thing that a system cannot possibly confront and remain itself, the place where it loops back on itself — which is really its origin, since a system is constituted by its looping back on itself — is this god? We could call it a fractal version of big-G God, who in any case is not a location — not like some supermassive black hole at the center of the universe — but something that's everywhere, something more like the capacity of the universe to form systems, or what might better be called the tendency or even the *desire* of the universe to do so.

For this reason, the reflexivity of consciousness doesn't just *represent* but actually *participates* in what I'm calling God here: *the loopiness of the universe.*

But if I could sit you down and explain God to you, so that you could say, *yes I understand,* and then just go about your business, how could that possibly be God? In fact, I've just done my best to explain — at least, the best I can muster at the moment — but did the clouds open up for you?

Well…a little, I said.

I'm afraid I'm more of a Virgil figure, said the Professor: I can lead you through Hell and Purgatory — like words themselves, that can only take you to the place where words fail. You need a Beatrice to bring you the rest of the way to experience "the love that moves the sun and other stars."

Fortunately, the inability of any explanation to deliver the experience, and the inability of any system to confront its own organizing principles — to tear out and hold in front of its eyes its own still-beating heart — isn't the end of the story.

Miraculous moments are moments when you come to terms with these organizing principles, when you *metabolize* them in some new way, even if you can't quite articulate them. The words of the lame philosopher may only be able to try to represent the world and to fall short — to die on the verge of the Promised Land — but the words of the poet seek not primarily to represent but to be alive and to participate — through their own reflexivity, their own loopiness — in the ways in which language itself is a form of life.

I thought the Professor had stolen the stuff about poetic language from me, but again I was flattered and let it pass.

If you were one of those people who divide people into two kinds (he continued), you could say that these are the two stances toward language: one fundamentally tragic and the other playful.

Well, if you must know (I said), I'm not one of those people who divide people into two kinds — but in case you thought you might be able to trick me into a contradiction, I'm also not one of those people who *don't* divide people into two kinds — and I'm not one of the All-of-the-Aboves, either: I'm a Both-and-Neither.

Okay, wiseguy (said the Professor), that just makes you one of the ones who divide people into *four* kinds.

The Professor's Divine Comedy analogy had triggered a long story that I couldn't resist telling him, a shaggy dog story, a series of detours, but also containing several relevant miracles and signs along the way.

VIII. Road Trip #1: The Story of Virgil

To begin at the end, in the manner of a eulogy: after almost 29 years and 163,000 miles, the forest-green 1970 Chevy Impala, sometimes known as Virgil, was laid to rest in August 1998 at Bobby Riordan's Automotive in Port Jefferson, New York, after a long illness. I had had the car for ten years. In fact, Virgil had been beyond repair since that February, when a routine inspection at Urban Classics of Brooklyn left the mechanic there, David Urbansky, unable to explain how the car was even running at all, in light of its many grave problems. But run Virgil did, until being driven — under his own power — to his final resting place. That was Virgil's final miracle — his eight cylinders, like a machinic menorah — kept on pumping for seven more months.

As Captain Reynolds said about his spaceship, "Love keeps her in the air when she oughta fall down."

Professor Lee had never seen that film. But he reminded me that this was — yet again — also the miracle I had claimed for my childhood leap: to have stayed in the air when I should have fallen down. Amazingly, again I hadn't even noticed this echo!

Anything that can be right in front of your nose without you noticing must be very important, the Professor said.

Anyway, I continued, it was Michel Serres — or maybe Bruno Latour — or in any case some French theorist — who observed that every organism is a "sheaf of times." This observation could have been inspired by the old Johnny Cash song about the car made up of parts from many different model-years.

The Professor knew that one.

Or you could say that Virgil's cross-country shuttlings back and forth were like the transits of a book-binder's needle, stitching together otherwise far-flung pages of lives and times.

Virgil's first owner was an old man who put only 40,000 miles on the car in eighteen years. The old man lived in Fargo, North Dakota, down the hall from my then-mother-in-law and above a funeral home. When he moved downstairs, she bought the car for me, from the old man's brother, for $1000.

In my 1997 book *Arrow of Chaos* — on page 53, in fact — I tell the story of how Virgil got his light-green-and-grey doors. This may be why a senior colleague of mine referred to the book as "a collection of fragments and personal anecdotes" — as if anything to do with this mythic vehicle could be reduced to the status of a mere personal anecdote!

Anyway, it was about a year later that my mother-in-law became my ex-mother-in-law, so I packed up Virgil and he and I moved from Minneapolis to San Francisco, "across the highways of America in tears," as Allen Ginsberg said in the poem *Howl*, a recording of which I played obsessively during that journey.

Professor Lee laughed. I can see this will be an uplifting story, he said. You telegraph that by the way you sugar-coat the bitter bits. So instead of saying the old man died, you say he moved downstairs, and instead of saying you got divorced from your wife, you say your mother-in-law became your ex-mother-in-law.

Those were *jokes*, I protested — but the Professor only said, *nevertheless.*

It was on this trip that Virgil got his name. Coming into San Francisco, over the Bay Bridge, I saw the city and the bridge-tops rising out of the mist, and I thought of the final words of the Inferno — "and we rose again to see the stars" — and it occurred to me that the car should be called Virgil: just as you said about the philosopher, he can't take you to Heaven, but he gets you through Hell. A few people also called him Vlad the Impala.

Virgil was with me for some other significant moments.

When the big quake hit San Francisco in 1989, I was just accelerating from a light in Menlo Park, just down the peninsula from the city. Virgil began to buck and sway. Suspecting a major transmission problem, I stopped immediately, right in the middle of an intersection, but the car kept on bucking and swaying, and I noticed that the light-poles all down the road were dancing like crazy and people were running out of buildings. Clearly a transmission problem of mythic proportions!

I remember passing with delight through the first snow of the year — a blizzard in the Rocky Mountains of Montana in early September, 1993 — while driving to Oregon with my friend Judith. That was where, at a rest stop overlooking badlands intermittently lit by distant lightning, we were amazed by a huge bison, just a few yards from us, who looked up from his grazing, seemed with mute approbation to recognize in the great grizzled green machine a kindred spirit, and bowed his head again to the grass.

The following summer, on Highway 50 in Nevada — known as "The World's Loneliest Highway" — Virgil received the cherished gift of some yellow desert wildflowers, which Iona had picked from the roadside. These flowers baked on his dashboard, next to a gold plastic crown, given to him by his old friend Judith. Iona's daughter Lang contributed a plastic mezuzah for his doorpost, and her son Nick found the four-character Chinese proverb that I stenciled in red above the front grill: *lao ma shi tao*: the old horse knows the way. It was always nice to see passing pedestrians smile when I was stopped at a light in Chinatown. And Virgil gave Clio and Isabella, Iona's son Liam's daughters, their first ride out into the world, from a hospital in Yonkers to their grandmother's house on Long Island.

But the times bound up in Virgil reach back further — like geologic strata — and forward — into the mists of futurity. Virgil's comings and goings stitched together "many a quaint and curious volume of forgotten lore." It's one of these stories that I want to tell now.

It begins for me in the summer of 1975. As yet unknown to me, Virgil was five years old and living a sedate life with the old man in Fargo.

I was eighteen and had just taken a bus from Boston to Boulder, Colorado, to visit a friend named Gina. The bus was run by a group called the Church of World Community Consciousness. They'd taken out the seats, so the passengers lolled around on the foam-rubber-padded floor. I arrived at Gina's with a woman named Teri, whom I'd met on the bus. None of this has much bearing on the story, but it gives some of the flavor of the times.

The first night in Boulder I dreamed that a large, writhing, irregular form was looming over the foot of the bed, trying to speak but only able to groan. Gina woke me from my own writhings and groanings. Much later I would write a poem in which the looming form was a ghost of my long-dead father, but I wasn't committed to this as an interpretation. I was just thinking of what Hamlet had said to his father's ghost: "Stay, illusion! If thou hast any sound, or use of voice, speak to me!"

Anyway, that evening, Gina, Teri and I went to hear Allen Ginsberg read *Howl* at the Naropa Institute, and the next day we drove up to Rocky Mountain National Park and ate some peyote. When I finished throwing up and the vice that felt like it was squeezing my head began to loosen a bit, we climbed a winding trail up the mountain. At one point, I stopped to rest, sprawling out on a large flat boulder by the side of the trail. Then we continued on to the top and walked onto a small glacier.

That glacier is probably gone by now.

Walking around on the ice, so magically cool in the hot sun, I forgot about how deathly ill I'd been feeling, and about my letdown that the peyote hadn't yielded even the slightest hallucination.

Coming back down the trail after an hour or so, we turned a corner and I saw, up ahead, the rock where I had stopped to rest — and saw, there on that rock, MYSELF, still sprawled there, waiting for our return!

The Professor smiled. Very Chinese of you, he said. Which is the real you; the one resting and waiting, or the one who pushes ahead and loops back?

Anyway, I said, I finally did return to Boulder fourteen years later, in 1989, with Virgil, on the trip to San Francisco I've already mentioned. The second day out of Minneapolis I got up very early and drove off toward Boulder in the misty morning. I was stopping there to visit my friend Kelly from graduate school — not the Kelly with whom Virgil and I were later to make half of an ill-fated cross-country trip, but the Kelly who would later marry Eric, who was himself at that time not yet divorced from Mayfair, who had been Iona's roommate at Peking University — but at this point I had never met Iona or Mayfair or Eric. None of these curious crossings of paths were yet marked on any map. Nor had I, on that misty morning — submerged as I was in the haze of present tears over the break-up of my marriage — thought anything of the time I'd been to Boulder so many years before.

The sun was beginning to burn off the morning mist as Virgil and I drove through the foothills. Suddenly, as we turned a corner, there was Boulder sprawled out below in the sunshine, laid out flat at the foot of the looming mountains. I thought of the dream I'd had that first night in Boulder fourteen years earlier and understood it in a flash, for the first time, at that instant: the darkly twisted, ancient, looming mountains, trying to speak; the blithely modern and sunlit city lying at their feet.

My own dream, as if it had been still resting there, waiting for me to return!

IX. Where God Comes From

The Professor liked the story, especially the uncanny doublings and parallels and the loopings back.

He observed that the punchline was another *materialized key*, this one to a forgotten riddle of the most interior sort: an ambiguous nocturnal shape in a dream. He liked the fact that the key turned out to be something diametrically opposed to the riddle: a mountain and a city — solid exterior realities laid out in front of me in the sunshine.

Now I want to tell you a story, he said. If I wanted to be portentous, I would say it was the master key that unlocks all the latent resonances in the stories you've been telling me, but I don't know if I can deliver that.

Did I tell you about the time I figured out where God comes

from?

I said it seemed like something I would have remembered.

I was on a city bus, the Professor said — in Portland, Oregon. I had been at a conference, stepped out for lunch, and just as I was walking past a bus stop somewhere in downtown Portland, a bus stopped next to me and the door opened, so on a whim I stepped in and paid the fare. I rode the bus out of town and got out and caught another bus back.

On the way back (and notice how this echoes all the loopings back in your stories, he said), I was thinking through the hypothesis that *loving something* means *attributing subjectivity to it*. Of course we habitually attribute subjectivity to people and things, even though it might be just as easy to think of them as objects, buffeted about by other forces — just as easy to locate subjectivity elsewhere, or nowhere.

But (I thought) doesn't one also attribute subjectivity to something one *hates*? And besides, *attributing* doesn't quite capture it. Manufacturing? Ventriloquizing? This was when I started thinking that this must be where God comes from.

Wait a minute, I protested — that's it? *That* was the big realization? Isn't that just a version of what Marx argued, that God is just a projected and alienated image of our own collective agency?

The Professor shook his head. This is just the first step. Subjectivization, entification: we tend to interact with things as if they were subjects, networks of forces as if they were discrete entities. It's a matter of attributive style. Anyway, you're making Marx into too much of a humanist. But we can come back to this. Be patient — let me tell you the rest.

I found myself taking a step back, thinking about myself thinking, and probably at least one more step back from that — but in any case, I quickly reached the highest level of metacognition I could attain — and I felt like I stumbled upon the actual limits of my own mind, which (as I've said) is something that, technically, one should not really be able to encounter at all.

There, sitting on a bus in Portland, among a motley crew of poor people, with (as it happened) Nina Simone singing "Blues for Mama" in my earphones (I don't know what it means, but that happened to be the soundtrack), watching the scenery roll by through my own ghostly reflection in the window, my thoughts rounded back upon themselves, and I discovered the actual edge of my world.

This is like what physicists mean when they say that the universe could be both finite and unbounded if it curves back on itself. You could keep going and going and never get to the end but find yourself back to where you'd been. Let's say that this was just a place where it curved a little more sharply, as if you were to walk around a corner and find yourself looking at the back of your own head.

You could try to say that what I came to the edge of wasn't the world at all but language and thought. As Wittgenstein said, "something beyond which we cannot go, and yet want to go, could not be the world." But here there was no question here of going beyond it or even wanting to go beyond it.

What I found there, at the end of the world, was not the terrifying, howling void I had visited at least a couple of times before —

Tell me about those times, I interrupted, but the Professor waved me off, quoting the Zohar: "When the Creator told Noah, 'The end of all flesh has come before me,' Noah asked, 'Which end?'"

Instead (the Professor continued), I felt myself gently pushed back, lovingly, by what I cannot say, back to what had been myself. I say "what had been myself" because, although on the one hand nothing had changed, I could also say that *the me that returned*, and *the me to whom I returned* had both been altered in the process.

Then I came back to where I'd been.
My room, it looked the same –
But there was nothing left between
The Nameless and the Named.

Then — and let me tell you the rest before I get back to whatever
it was that pushed me back in such a loving way — this made me
remember another moment, the moment where I overcame the
fear of death, when I realized that what I actually feared was the
shame—eternal flames of hell in the moment of dying—for
breaking the most fundamental social contract to keep on
living—and then realized that one might avoid such a breach
simply by breathing the simplest and most famous of last words:
goodbye.

He stopped for a moment.

Do you see how similar this is to your mockingbird
experience? The loving hand or eye that reflects you back to
yourself and changes you in the process — the revelation that
occurs in the moment of looping back — the doublings and
echoes?

I recognized it all, and I was beginning to get the feel of what
the Professor liked to call the cognitive and emotional architecture of complexity. But (I said), even if the sublimity could
give people goosebumps, this is not what most people would
recognize as God, at least in my neck of the woods, where He is
thought to be an elderly gentleman with long grey hair and a
beard who likes to float around in a white bathrobe, surrounded
by winged babies. The one you pray to.

Well, said the Professor, I didn't say it was God. I said it was
where God comes from.

That's a lot worse, I replied. God isn't supposed to come from
anywhere — everything is supposed to come from God. Sounds
like you're one of the haters and deflaters — one of those who
say that God is just a grandiose projection of Mommy and

Daddy, with their unconditional love and punishments, or God is a temporal lobe disturbance, or a meme that stuck in our brains and got conserved because it helps produce social cohesion.

Look, said the Professor, I've got no particular quarrel with any of these explanations — inflated parent, synaptic ghost, social glue — all fine, though obviously too reductive — but at the same time, I also don't object to various personalizations of God — an old guy with a beard, or a wafer or whatever — again, all good, but obviously reductive. Or if you want to go in the No Graven Images direction — that makes sense to me too.

The problem with God as a concept, as far as I'm concerned, is exactly the same as the problem with evolution or a mechanistic universe as concepts: the reductive way they get used to take what has arisen through miraculously complex interrelationships and cast it as something boringly familiar that doesn't ruffle our one-size-fits-all grammar of subjects, verbs and objects and our notions of agency and purpose. In other words, the problem is *not* in how we use god or evolution or mechanism as ways of thinking about these things but *as ways not to think about them.*

In any case, even the most religious aren't saying that the word *God* or our concept or personification of God or even a transubstantiated wafer is the totality of God. In all of these cases, there's something prior to the word or the concept or the instantiation — it comes from somewhere. I'm just saying that we can't fully wrap our minds around the wrapping that constitutes our minds. But I'm also saying that the concept and the word have some real connection to whatever precedes them, and that it is something miraculous that we can only glimpse. You can make me sound as religious or as anti-religious as you like.

So (I asked), what about the loving hand that pushed you back — and why was *that* what you found at the end of the world at that moment, instead of a howling void?

Well, he said, that was just because I happened to be thinking about love at the time.

I was irritated by this. I said it seemed to me that whenever I was feeling cynical or suspicious of what the Professor was saying, he held out the prospect of something sublime, but whenever he had me poised for sublimity, he burst the bubble with something like this, something pedestrian and unremarkable. Was this some trick he learned in Zenmaster School, or what?

Alright, wiseguy, he said, let me explain it another way. Just as there can be mutual negation and meta-negation to infinity, there can be love and meta-love to infinity as well — like valleys and peaks of an emotional and cognitive landscape. But you have to try to set aside the false opposition of the sublime and the pedestrian.

But then some thought seemed to provoke him, and he practically shouted at me: so why are you here visiting me? Maybe the rock just under the surface of your mind — is *me*. You don't see anyone else here, do you? They're all doing other things. But you swam out to me. You tell me; what is just below the surface or beyond the edge of your mind?

I saw what he meant — or I should say, the emotional intensity of the way he said it brought it home to me.

It was about love. That's why I'm here.

X. The Pedestrian Sublime

Time is peculiarly chopped up . . .; only a few days open up, they are significant ones. (Walter Benjamin)

This conversation with Professor Lee, which I have only very artificially recreated here, touched off a rhizomic network in my brain that has continued to cause wildflowering thoughts to spring up in assorted unexpected places. This book is a bunch of them.

Thinking back on it, I have occasionally felt embarrassed that

I'd thought of such fussy little miraculous moments instead of more melodramatic ones — like falling in love and fucking and the bed catching on fire at a climactic moment, or spinning around twice in a car, with my then-wife, at 50 miles an hour on an icy freeway bridge over the Mississippi River and walking away without a scratch (although shortly thereafter we divorced, and years later the bridge itself collapsed!), or meeting my half-sister for the first time, by chance, in a public library.

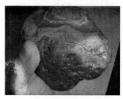

Or it would occur to me that the miraculous is not limited to the intricately layered little nuggets — that is, the agates (for which I will admit a fondness, ever since I was a kid) — nor the high drama (to which I am also sometimes attracted). There are also moments when, even though you can't point to any particular set of emotional or cognitive or dramatic factors, everything just seems to *glow*. And thinking about this range of the miraculous, I can sometimes get the sense that it is coextensive with the landscape of our world, that our whole lives are woven of miracle. Professor Lee, I think — for whatever reasons — had figured out how more continuously to inhabit this feeling.

I also began to think of his assertion that daily life and the sublime are not necessarily opposed, but rather than spreading out over my life and planting a permanent Mona Lisa smile on my face, it made me focus more on a particular experience I'd had years earlier.

It happened when I visited the Alps for the first time in April, 2002, with my old friend Alex, who was living in Geneva at the time. We walked up a trail from the French village of Sixt Fer à Cheval. We ambled through valleys and scrambled up rocky slopes, along the edge of a glacier, through woods and pastures peppered with wildflowers, alongside a rushing stream, up to a broad and desolate cirque — an amphitheater-shaped depression at the top of the mountain — where we were surprised to find a rustic restaurant serving croissants and lemonade — but this was France, after all.

We had left in the morning and got back down again to the village just before sunset, but the flat evenness of clock-time seemed to have been radically tilted and opened up along with the terrain. I remember thinking over and over along the way, I can't believe I am allowed to be here, to experience this.

At one point the trail branched out into several smaller paths along a steep slope. I can't recall if we were walking up or down, or whether Alex or I had gone ahead, but I had been walking alone for a while. I came to a place where a little stream had spread out from its channel to flow down over a broad, smooth expanse of rock. There across the rock mottled with mosses and scattered wildflowers, the water flowed into a thousand sparkling shapes—trickles, burbling rivulets, and sheets of water—all continuously separating and recombining as they flowed over the rock face, just as a vast pilgrimage would make its way across uneven terrain.

Maybe on another day I would have walked by without paying much attention. After all, it was just water doing what water does, flowing downhill in whatever way it can. Maybe it was because what the water was doing seemed to echo the multiple paths into which the trail had split, and because Alex and I also had been splitting up and rejoining with each other in the course of our hike, and because, in the larger sense, our lives have been so multiple and so intertwined, having diverged and rejoined so many times as now to seem to have been strands of one life all along. Maybe there is always this fractal quality to mystical experience, this resonance between different scales and dimensions, this translucence of the universal and the specific.

It also struck me at the time that what the water was doing was also the story that physics tells about the universe, how it flows down the spacetime gradient from the singular peak of the Big Bang, perhaps down all the way to the featureless plain known as "heat death" (when all matter will have dissolved into a uniform mist in which not even protons remain). Along the way, the flow eddies into myriad shapes, generating other gradients with their own eddies, the "nonequilibrium thermodynamic systems" that surf the gradients: galaxies and stars and you and I.

XI. A Web of Meandering Connections

I wonder how much my experience that day may have been scripted by the Romantic poetry I've studied and taught for so long, which famously hypes the sublimity of the Alps.

Not far from where I was walking, Percy Shelley stood, in 1816, in the Valley of Chamounix, looking down from a bridge at the Arve River, which he imagined flowing down from a "secret throne" at the top of Mont Blanc, carving a path of ongoing creation and destruction as it goes, through its "many-coloured, many-voiced vale."

Shelley's poem echoes Coleridge's earlier poem "Kubla Khan," the record of an opium dream in which Coleridge imagined a sacred river gushing out from a violent spring "with ceaseless turmoil seething," then "meandering with a mazy motion / Through wood and dale" as it makes its way through the zone inhabited by humans before plunging again into sublime depths "through caverns measureless to man / Down to a sunless sea."

Although thermodynamics as such wouldn't be developed until later in the nineteenth century, Coleridge seems to have had some kind of imagistic grasp of it. The contrasts built into his imagined "sunny pleasure dome with caves of ice" mark the dynamic balance of forces necessary to create a habitable zone on the "edge of chaos." No doubt much of Coleridge's understanding came from his experience of the predicament of a psyche teetering precariously, far from equilibrium, between the "ceaseless turmoil" of mania and the infinitely deep and "sunless sea" of his depression.

And by the way, Coleridge's radar was also uncanny in fixing on Kubla Khan, who is now suspected to have been a fellow addict and depressive, at least in the last years of his life. Kubla suffered the loss of his favorite wife and of the son he had chosen as his successor, conspicuous failures in expansionist campaigns in Japan and southeast Asia, and assorted rebellions in his own domains: his world was coming apart at the seams. Like a thirteenth-century Elvis, Kubla began to eat and drink heavily, became grotesquely fat, and turned to drugs and shamans, but "nothing produced relief, and the eating and drinking binges continued" until, "extremely dispirited and depressed," he died in 1294. I don't know if it loomed very large among his many troubles, but it seems particularly poignant to me (and curiously modern) that Kubla's daughter Miao Yen had become a Buddhist nun, worshipping Kuan-yin. The great granddaughter of Ghengis Khan worshipped the Goddess of Mercy (so the story goes) "day and night with such fervor that the marks of her forehead and her feet may be traced on the flagstone" of her monastery.

In any case — as Professor Lee taught me to understand — my experience on the mountain was not the grandiose and melodramatic sublime of the Romantic Alps but more of a quotidian sublime, a *pedestrian sublime*. The texture of the moment was not really very different from any other moment, though I was in a better mood, and the sunshine was crisper and the air clearer. And it wasn't tied to Romantic notions of the restorative powers of Nature, either. In fact, a few years later, I had a very similar experience in the Times Square subway station in New York City, about as far from an Alpine mountaintop as you can get.

Again I was walking, this time between trains, down a broad corridor in the midst of crowds flowing continuously in opposite directions *through each other*, and continuously separating and recombining as crowds do through myriad complex and instantaneous social negotiations, all seemingly orchestrated with the steady rolling blues pumping into my brain through my earphones. The mostly laminar flow of the crowds became more turbulent when the corridor opened up into a vast atrium with other corridors, turnstiles, and stairways on all sides, people going every which way. Along one wall a crowd two or three people deep had congealed around a couple of identical-twin flamenco guitarists, the proud and emphatic strains of flamenco breaking through my steady rolling blues.

At other times, in other moods, and maybe even with other combinations of music, the same station can be a nightmare; cacophonous, assaultive, overwhelming. I know people who have moved away from New York City just to escape this kind of daily jostling with crowds in subways, and I have to admit that crowds most often make me anxious at some basic kinetic and neurological level. It is one of the defining experiences of urban modernity that Walter Benjamin found so important for Baudelaire. But on that day, I found moving with so many others moving, oceanic; being both a part of and apart from them all, so plural and singular.

XII. Keats and Kauffman

And now, in the now of writing about this experience after having just thought of the Romantic poets, I am reminded of a Keats letter from 1819:

> This it is that makes the Amusement of Life—to a specu-
> lative Mind. I go among the Fields and catch a glimpse of a
> stoat or a fieldmouse peeping out of the withered grass—
> the creature hath a purpose and its eyes are bright with it—
> I go amongst the buildings of the city and I see a Man
> hurrying along—to what? The Creature has a purpose and
> his eyes are bright with it.

Not one merely to elevate himself from among his fellow creatures as a privileged observer, Keats adds another layer to the image:

> I myself am pursueing the same instinctive course as the veriest human animal you can think of—I am however young writing at random—straining at particles of light in the midst of a great darkness . . .. May there not be some superior beings amused with any graceful, though instinctive attitude my mind may fall into, as I am entertained with the alertness of a stoat or the anxiety of a Deer?

Here is that fractal quality again. In Keats's letter, it seems to be organized mostly into a series of vertical levels—a pyramidal kind of hierarchy sometimes known as the Great Chain of Being: in this case, the stoat (a kind of weasel) is watched by the poet, who is watched in turn by superior beings. This hierarchical way of thinking was still prevalent in Keats's time, in the throes of a very uneven and ongoing transition from a quasi-feudal social hierarchy that still seemed to color all things. But there is also at least the hint of something more horizontal and network-like about Keats's image, a web of observers who are also being observed by others in the web — a very modern or even postmodern image. The eyes of the hyper-alert stoat and the anxiously vigilant deer are bright, presumably, with the instinctive purpose of *observation*. This already undermines any implicit opposition between instinctive, unreflective purposeful activity and disinterested, meditative observation.

To complicate further any too-easy distinction between base instincts and higher callings, Keats goes on to propose the image of an "ellectric fire in human nature" that burns in everyone so that "among these human creatures there is continually some birth of new heroism" as if, every so often, the conditions are right for some flames to leap a little higher, and not because these flames are somehow morally superior to other flames but because this is just what fire does. Water flows down, just as lighter-than-air flames leap up. We do not think of either as *striving* but as quite the opposite of striving; as following the path of least resistance, as equilibrium-seeking, going with the flow, doing something easy without trying at all, "like falling off a log" as the saying goes.

This goes with the growing realization in biology that life is not wildly improbable but an "expected *emergent collective property* of a modestly complex mixture of catalytic polymers" as physicist Stuart Kauffman puts it. This realization has begun to displace the dominant notion of evolution as "climbing Mount Improbable," life swimming upstream, heroically battling the forces of disorder as it wrests ever more intricate order from the jaws of chaos. As already noted, societies tend to see their own images in the mirror of nature. Just as the hierarchical Great Chain of Being is a holdover from a feudal social hierarchy, this much more dynamic but still hierarchical notion of life swimming upstream is a holdover from the nineteenth-century imperial white ruling-class notion of itself as pursuing its civilizing mission while beset on all sides by the "powers of darkness."

To change this notion of heroic striving means changing a whole interlinked constellation of metaphors that are key points of reference not only in science but in western culture generally. We think of striving up and falling down, and it is almost as if to change this way of thinking would be as disorienting as a loss of gravity. Would things start falling up? Would one have to struggle to stay down?

We tend to think of purposeful activity as difficult (and sometimes as noble or morally superior) and relaxation as easy, but think of how difficult it is to lie down and rest when you're bursting with energy—and how climbing down is often harder than climbing up. We tend to think of complexity as difficult to achieve and to understand, while simplicity is easy, but think of how hard it is to put into simple words the thoughts or feelings whose complexity came so easily to us in the first place. We tend to think of "going with the flow" as a slacker's creed, but what if the flow is turbulent, traversing uneven terrain, constantly forming into crashing waves and swirling eddies as it gushes up over rocks and plummets down waterfalls?

You tell me, is your life more like drifting down a lazy river or shooting the rapids?

A couple days after I wrote about standing on the mountainside among the rivulets, which was a few years after the event, I found that my memory of that day had been taken over almost completely by my written account, and I felt a sense of loss and betrayal. I felt that by writing about the experience I had sold it out, trampled through its twining wildflowers in big word-boots. But when I returned to it a few weeks later, the written account had become part of that earlier event after all, really an event in progress, a constellation of events still in the process of constellating.

The experience had been an event in the first place because it was not an isolated moment but an event in process, an especially resonant node in a network of events.

People like to say that all we have is the present and that the past and future don't really exist. It seems to me that it's more like the other way around. The present is the only thing that doesn't really exist; it's a fictional zero-dimensional point in a fabric made of a series of strands that are events; strands of meaning whose weave is responsible for continuity, repetition, difference, *pattern* that plays out only across time, from past to future.

Time, and the world along with it, is a sail, a set of exquisite riggings, that catches the quantum wind blowing continually through the void of the present.

This notion also seems to have a particular neurological

reality. According to psychologists like Daniel Stern, our sense of a "present moment" tends to have a duration of several seconds; Francisco Varela calls this a "window of simultaneity." Of course, our experience of time is not a succession of present moments tied together like a string of sausages. It's more like a kind of fabric in which these short fibers are pressed together with multiple overlaps, like *felt* — which is why I like the phrase *felt experience*.

Moments are not punctual; they are not the elemental particles of time. For example, it couldn't be just that "an image popped into my mind" — moments have architecture, orchestration — "I was walking along, looking at the scenery, when an image popped into my mind" — and while they have many kinds of connections to other moments and other dimensions of experience, they also have a finite duration — "and then the image faded when I remembered something else." In mystical experience, one may speak of an expanded or heightened present, or of the sense of a present overwhelmed by its resonances with past and future; that is, with *meaning*. Remembering our hike, for example, I feel that our ascent and descent was all part of a single experience.

And now—if I can still use that word, *now* — you are reading these words, these very words, linking them with your own thoughts with their own networks of resonances. What happened to me on a mountaintop in the Alps and under the streets of New York City, along with all the books I read — all the cosmology and poetry that resonated with these events for *me* — whoever was the writer of these lines — along with *you* — whatever has brought you here, to be reading these words right now, and whatever is going on in your mind now, all your resonances, right now — are also part of this constellation.

Did you notice that these experiences — walking in the mountains and in the subway station — *like writing and reading* — are about being simultaneously alone and connected with others?

Whatever else it's about, every book also has to be an exercise in writing and reading. Everything is what it is, not just something instrumental, not just a means to some other end. Language isn't just a black-and-white window onto a colorful world beyond (reading as instrumental and representational), but it isn't just a geode with inward-facing crystals (reading for its own sake) either. It's a node in a resonant network.

Chapter Two

Beginnings

I. Are We Being Hustled by God?

It's common sense that simplicity comes first and that complexity grows out of it.

This narrative is enshrined in what sometimes goes by the name of Romanticism, often involving nostalgia for the so-called "simple days" of childhood, or adolescence, or young adulthood, or of a time of national innocence (when was that, exactly?), a time of unselfconsciousness, before we were burdened down by layers of self-consciousness, reflection, shame, guilt and second-guessing.

Various kinds of anti-Romanticisms, such as the movement in philosophy known as *deconstruction*, seek to overturn these narratives. Deconstruction began by targeting the notion, which seems to be very close to the core of Western thought, that opposes speech and writing. Speech, in this notion, gets valued as simple presence in the moment, while writing has typically been cast as a shady supplement, associated with multiple layers of meaning and the ambiguous play of presence and absence. Can you even tell how many people wrote the words you are now reading? Is the writer of these words even alive? Historically, writing has been allied with complexity.

But the notion of beginning with the simple seems to be rooted in something beyond religion or ideology or philosophy, something more solid than a dominant paradigm — something fundamental, universal, unquestionable. After all, aren't humans more complex than fish, and fish more complex than amoebas? Overall, isn't the current teeming ecosystem ever more complex than where it began, with some few quivering molecules in a puddle of inorganic slime on a rocky planet? And isn't the universe, with all of its emergent processes and structures — gravity and gamma rays and galaxies and grammar — more complex than the dimensionless point of the Big Bang, where it all began?

Even these narratives are theories, shaped (or at least colored) by various ideological or historical constraints. We can make it even more basic: isn't one simpler than two, and two simpler than three? Complexity can't just spring from nothingness; it has to come from somewhere. Before there is two, there is first one and then another one added to it. *Right?*

Well, part of the problem is that to think the simple we have to be able to think in the first place, and to be able to think at all is to be a very complex creature in a very complex universe.

But even in our very complex world, or so one might argue, the simple continues to precede the complex; it is a continual feature of *emergence* generally. A human baby, though already a very complex creature, still has to babble before talking and to learn to write a halting word or two before attempting the Great American Novel. But this is a much trickier argument than it seems. The "platform" on which all of humanity and human society and culture are being built is already hypercomplex — and babbling, talking and writing are all unthinkable without such a platform. Instead of believing that all new things begin simply and have always done so, we might get the idea instead that all new things, including simple ones, emerge from a matrix of already-existing complexity.

Professor Lee wanted me to call this condition "having a mother." At first, I protested that it would undermine the argument, practically inviting people to dismiss it as an artifact of my own personal psychopathology, something manufactured to compensate for my own mother-deficit. And, as I had done many times, I pointed out the irony of his always wanting me to reveal more about my personal life in my writing, when he would not even allow his real name (or anything else about him) to appear in print!

Of course, any theorist with any self-awareness knows that all theory is autobiography at some level, but you have to go to the next level of awareness to realize that a theorist is someone equipped to question things that other people take for granted, someone for whom a whole category of things or a certain condition are deeply problematic, since someone who takes for granted the category or condition is not going to be driven to theorize them. Various deficits and deviancies do not disqualify you from being a theorist — they're *prerequisites*.

In any case, the conundrum of whether to begin with simplicity or complexity is at the heart of one of the biggest questions in physics. If the universe began in a single point, as the Kabbalah tells us—I mean, as modern physics has theorized — how did the particles and relationships and laws come to evolve as they did and not some other way — or not at all? How did the parameters of the universe come to be "tuned" as they are? Or to adapt an old, familiar metaphor: when the cosmic cue-ball was sent off with a mighty thwack, and started rolling down the table and began to spin ever so slightly, curving more and more, was the symmetry-breaking simple chance, or was there something in that thwack, some "English" to begin with? Or to put the question in extreme figurative shorthand, are we being hustled by God?

It is not at all clear that you have to have one before you can have two. Let's say one is like a single particle, and then as other particles are added, they begin to form a numbering system, a set of relationships. This is like saying that noun-like things are first, and verbs and grammar follow as nouns begin to pile up. But wait. Don't relationships come FIRST? Don't you have to have numbers in order to have "one" at all?

Modern Western thought is fond of the myth of the social contract, the proposition that individuals got together to form society. But where did the individuals come from? Did they just wander out of their caves, squinting and rubbing their eyes, stumbling into some clearing, where they encountered others for the first time? No! They had to have mothers, didn't they? And their mothers were not alone, either. They probably got together regularly to play mahjong. In fact, society is the *precondition* for individuals.

There have always been tensions in the West between and among the notion of a single god, or no god, or multiple gods (from three all the way up to pantheistic infinity). The Christian trinity seems to be a kind of syncretistic compromise; three-in-one.

My old pal William Blake, who invented his own new-age myth, posited an original four-fold god. The trouble begins (according to Blake) when one of the four tries to take over and become the supreme deity, producing a backlash of assorted convulsive divisions and emanations in which other entities (deities and eventually people) multiply like mad. Western scientific rationality was always charged with the thunderingly intolerant, monotheistic fervor it borrowed from the Judeo-Christian tradition: thou shalt have no other alternative rationalities before me! That was Blake's point.

The philosopher Willard Quine had an ecological — or as many people say, wholistic — view of thinking: our theories and paradigms are more stable and unassailable the more networked they are with other theories and paradigms. The most difficult idea to topple is the most connected, the most *nodal*, since toppling it would necessitate reworking all the other ideas dependent on it. And ideas, by the way, don't just float around in the ether; they're hooked up to material networks of practices, institutions, disciplines, even synaptic structures in our brains. When a really nodal theory is threatened (by competing theories or by troublesome evidence), it's usually easier just to do damage control. The most famous example is the earth-centered universe, which was kept running with various conceptual bendings-over-backwards—in addition to prosecutions and persecutions of nay-sayers — way beyond its expected sell-by date.

The notion that simplicity is first is probably just about as massively networked as the earth-centered universe. It is supported by its relatives in ideology (various forms of Romanticism), scientific method (reductionism), religious and national myth (the "loss of innocence" narrative), and so on. It is so well connected that, when you find any little crack in it and stick a crowbar in there and begin working it back and forth a little, you can feel the whole structure groaning and creaking. That's what I've been starting to do here. Argumentative form really is more physical than anything else: you try to find a little crack, you push one way and then the other, push and then ease off, push again and then ease off.

Right now I'm easing off. Can you feel it?

One way and then another, like a crowbar. Or say instead, adapting the image, that the mind is like a bloodhound tracking an elusive scent, zig-zagging diagonally across the track. Like eyes scanning back and forth across the night sky to glimpse stars the fixed gaze misses. Like switchbacks that make an otherwise too-steep slope walkable. Like a sailboat tacking against the wind, if you want to make it sound hard — or if you prefer to make it sound easy, like water finding its own weaving way down a mountainside.

Woosh! Woosh! Woosh!

II. Dumb Luck Versus Intelligent Design

"Not chess, Mr. Spock: *poker*." (Captain James T. Kirk)

A while back, after years of being an inconsistent poker player, I finally figured out why people like me lose at poker.

Here's how it works: they think, "I probably won't get the card I need to win this hand, but I'm gonna stay in anyway," and then they think, "come on king of hearts, come on, come on, come on." Then when the three of clubs turns up, they think, "shit! What was I thinking?"

The problem is not that they don't know the odds but that they'd rather be lucky than intelligent. Why? It's about love.

Luck, which in the West tends to be linked to the Christian concept of god's grace, is how the universe shows that it loves you unconditionally: sure, kid, I'll give you the king of hearts! And it's not that you did anything to deserve or not deserve it, which is what makes it sweet.

It's very different if you win after ascertaining the odds of your drawing the card you need and the probabilities of other players' hands, the likelihood of being able to bluff successfully, and so on. In this model, the universe doesn't necessarily care for you, but *you must care for it* in the sense that you must learn its implacable ways and look for ways to leverage these to your own advantage. (I can hear Professor Lee saying, I see you're still talking about your relationship with your mother!) Note that this approach can be called both very selfish, since the calculations are all about maximizing one's own advantage, and also very unselfish and other-directed, since it involves intense and sustained focus — I want to say *loving attention* — on something other than oneself.

Science seems to promote this intense and sustained focus on coming to know the world, the better to serve our own advantage. At its best, science is a way of loving the world. And does the world love us back? What would that mean in scientific terms?

The usual narrative is that science shows us, above all else, that in spite of all of what our own narcissism makes us feel, we are not at the center of the universe. This is why the game-changing discovery that the earth revolves around the sun — in spite of manifest visual evidence to the contrary — is taken as exemplary of the kind of de-centering that science does. It shows us how small and insignificant we are, that nature is no respecter of persons, that a series of accidents enabled us to emerge, and that any number of accidents could wipe us out at any moment (but in any case, that things are likely to end very badly), and so on. You could put a Buddhist spin on this, but to catch the real flavor of early science in the West, you've got to paint it with sufficient Protestant grimness. Just as life battled every inch of the way through luck and pluck and bucking the odds against the forces of disorder represented by the Second Law of Thermodynamics, so science and reason strive ever upward against the forces of superstition and ignorance that continue to surround them on all sides — so the story goes.

However far we've come since the early days of science, the dominance of this paradigm is such that it may seem vaguely theological to assert that we are "at home in the universe" (as Stuart Kauffman has done) and that, far from being an uphill struggle, life comes as easily to the universe as quarks and atoms and galaxies. Even entertaining the notion that complexity could come first makes it seem like one might be positing an intelligence that precedes everything, and thus sneaking God back in.

So, to pull back a bit and try to avoid tripping the science/religion polarity, let's try a gentle exploration of the question of whether complexity is built into the universe or to what extent it has arisen from originally simple laws and conditions.

Physicist Murray Gell-Mann takes the position that complexity arises from simplicity through what he calls "frozen accidents," defined as random convergences that turn out to have "widespread consequences for the future."

The image of the "frozen accident" is an odd one, since what we are talking about is *a fortuitous key event that sets other events in motion*, really the opposite of something frozen. I'm more inclined to imagine it as the wake of a ship, a consequence that is literally *widespread*. The notion also recalls ancient philosopher Lucretius's account of the original fall of atoms like rain through the void of empty space, until some begin to swerve ever so slightly and to converge and form clusters. "If it were not for this swerve," writes Lucretius, "nature would never have created anything." This might also bring to mind what has been called the Butterfly Effect, whereby some tiny, fleeting event can trigger massive, systemic effects. Notice that these images of fleeting perturbations -- swerving raindrops, flapping butterflies — are the opposite of what is usually meant by "frozen."

In order to come to the image of a frozen accident, one first must imagine a gas or liquid, a wanton soup of particles in ongoing random movement. Something happens — a temperature drop, or the introduction of some catalyst — and a kind of freezing or crystallization occurs. This freezing involves the linkage of particles with each other, the emergence of relationality, regularity and structure from randomness. Like other coming-into-relation narratives, this one fails to recognize that its characters—particles in random motion — were already congealed relationships to begin with.

As Gell-Mann puts it, in a rather convoluted way, "a 'frozen accident' produces a great deal of mutual algorithmic information among various parts or aspects of a future coarse-grained history of the universe, for many such histories and for various ways of dividing them up."

To put it more straightforwardly, such accidents *make things matter to each other* — and by the way, this is a big part of what can otherwise be called *meaning*.

To take an obvious example, the rise of carbon-based life on Earth has had very dramatic consequences for the geo-chemical organization of the planet's surface. It guarantees that this geochemical organization will be all-important for us (and when I say *us*, I'm speaking for the moment only to other carbon-based lifeforms—my apologies to the rest of you). It links our histories and our futures. Carbon and oxygen matter to us very much, and at least in our own neighborhood of space and time, we matter very much to them. And notice that the extent of this linkage is not given in advance. The organisms that came before us reorganized the elements of the Earth's surface and produced its atmosphere in a way that enabled us to emerge, but how in turn will we reorganize it? Our own fate as well as that of the distribution of elements on and around the planet's surface hang in the balance. (At least until the sun goes supernova and…there goes the neighborhood. After all, as Gell-Mann puts it, frozen accidents are "restricted to particular regions of space and time.")

Gell-Mann explains that, "as time goes by in the history of the universe and accidents (with probabilities for various outcomes) accumulate, so do frozen accidents, giving rise to regularities," and thus, "as the universe grows older and frozen accidents pile up, the opportunities for effective complexity to increase keep accumulating as well. Thus there is a tendency for the envelope of complexity to expand even though any given entity may either increase or decrease its complexity during a given time period."

So there you have it, the secret of the universe and of life, revealed in four little words: "frozen accidents pile up," or FAPU, for short. It's the flip side of "things fall apart" (otherwise known as the Second Law of Thermodynamics): yes they do, but FAPU too. Everything interesting in the universe, then, is a String of Frozen Accidents; a SOFA. According to this image, we start with randomness and the simple laws of physics, and accidents begin to produce clusters—piles—or linkages—strings—and, ultimately, networks of strings — webs. The image of freezing was an image of linkage in the first place—a single frozen accident is already a kind of "pile-up." Since this makes complex order a Pile of Piles, let's call this the POP theory.

But this is really just a way of defining order in the first place, coupled with a commitment to this order not being original but having emerged from an original disorder. And notice how the image of heaps of frozen things marks a commitment to the hard, macho, pre-biological world of physics: no weaving of webs or fabrics here, and definitely no butterflies!

On the other hand, biologist Harold Morowitz defines frozen accidents as "random events that so alter the system that their effects persist." Clearly, this contradicts Gell-Mann's definition. Morowitz's version requires one first to imagine not randomness but a system, subject to random accidents, some of which will become part of the system. This is what Blake meant when he wrote "substance gives tincture to accident and makes it physiognomic." Not surprisingly, Morowitz's exemplary case is genetic mutation. So let's call this theory the Mutational (or Morowitzian) Organizational Matrix, or MOM for short (and a gold star to those of you who saw that coming from a mile away).

I once worked at a university where, no matter what kind of program you were proposing, you couldn't even get in the Provost's door unless you had a good acronym. He simply didn't have time for complex intellectual rationales. Never mind all that! What's your *acronym*? I'm going with MOM and POP Theory.

Evolutionist Daniel Dennett comes down firmly on Gell-Mann's side when he asserts, in one of his responses to the Intelligent Design dogma, that "the designs found in nature are nothing short of brilliant, but the process of design that generates them is utterly lacking in intelligence of its own." This is a defensive statement — a reactionary statement. What it's trying to defend against is of course that old bogey, an anthropo-morphized god, the Designer God of Intelligent Design.

But by the same token, notice that this defense also operates against anything that might jeopardize the exceptional and uniquely privileged status of humanity; the notion that intelli-gence belongs to us alone. This exceptionalism has a Judeo-Christian genealogy too, and it is closely related to the heroic story of order and eventually human life emerging and developing against the grain of an entropic universe.

If this scientific exceptionalism has a religious pedigree, it is worth noting too that Intelligent Design vies with classical rationalism for reductionism, short-circuiting all of what is most miraculous and mysterious about the universe, namely the very open and even mystical question of the emergence of complex order, and offering instead an explanation short enough to be printed on a t-shirt: only God could have made it.

So it seems that a reversal of the old formula may be apt: religion, with its brutal reductionism, would squash all the awesome miracles — and the loving attention to the world — that science opens up for us.

In response both (on the one hand) to the attribution of intelligence to an anthropomorphic god and (on the other) to the defensive assertion that intelligence belongs to humans alone, a very simple opening gambit seems appropriate: that the prevalence of recursive processes in nature constitute something we might as well call intelligence, since just such processes characterize consciousness.

Or if you prefer the glass-half-empty version (I don't, but in case you do), since it seems that our own consciousness is more of a piece with other chemical and biological processes, it appears that our prodigious and godly intelligence has been, well — *overrated*.

III. Claymation

...people named Dennis do, in fact, gravitate toward dentistry. (*Journal of Personality and Social Psychology*)

One of the authors [of] a paper on allergic airways inflammation in *The American Journal of Respiratory and Critical Care Medicine* . . . is Takamichi Ichinose of the National

Institute for Environmental Studies, Tsukuba, Japan. (*New Scientist*)

Keats said of Shakespeare's sonnets that "they seem to me to be full of fine things said unintentionally—in the intensity of working out conceits" — *conceits* being an old word for extended metaphors.

How could this happen, that metaphors would seem to operate on their own, beyond the control of even the greatest master of language? Or should we say instead that the greatest master is one who can *allow* this to happen?

It is widely acknowledged that scientific metaphors are to some extent normative, meaning that they help shape thought and action via the theoretical frameworks in which they participate. What interests me even more here is how metaphor also seems so embody crucial tensions and contradictions in scientific theory. Either way, it's about how they seem to *take on a life of their own*.

The chemist A.G. Cairns-Smith famously postulated that simple metabolic processes may have arisen chemically, in microcrystalline structures of clay, before being "taken over" by emergent genes: metabolism first, then genes. To illustrate how this paradigm differs from the usual accounts, he uses a pointedly working-class metaphor:

> There is another way of looking at an organisation: not through the boardroom, through *the control structure*, but at the lay-out on the factory floor. Not by asking the question 'What is needed to control what?' but by asking instead 'What is needed to make what?' We can call this *the supply structure* of an organisation.

There is something to say about the scientific value of this metaphor even if, as outsiders, we can't assess directly the validity of the theory. The priority accorded to the genome is thoroughly shaped by capitalist ideology: genes are understood as control structures or managerial entities. They deal in information and direct other entities who are, effectively, the biological laboring classes. Even in terms of the most naïve scientific realism, we would have to say that such a historically specific framework — and exacerbating that, such a thorough-going class bias — makes for bad science, or at least very constrained science. To this we might further observe that, anytime *unmarked* metaphors are used — that is, metaphors used without systematic mindfulness to their bias and baggage — we would expect that these would be likely to conform to dominant ideology. In this sense at least, we can say that Cairns-Smith's metaphor makes for better science.

The practical conclusion is even more obvious: scientists should keep scholars of poetics on the payroll to help them work with metaphors.

A more famous example is the metaphor of the tree of life, in which creatures are represented as evolving and diversifying outward like branches from some single ancient ancestor. This is an explicitly patriarchal image, since family trees are only tree-shaped because they start with a patriarch and are organized by patriarchal family names — otherwise there would be no trees in sight, just a complex and multidimensional web. Problem is, the tree-of-life metaphor drastically constrains thinking. For example, it does not allow one to imagine creatures actually merging together; in fact, it makes this seem like an abomination or an impossibility. Maybe this is why it took a woman, biologist Lynn Margulis, to discover that every cell of our bodies is the product of such a merger long ago in the evolutionary web! This is why the mitochondria in each of our cells have *different* DNA than we do.

Of course Cairns-Smith spends no time considering the gender and class bias of scientific metaphors — he can't afford to be mistaken for a literary critic, after all! He simply represents his metabolism-first theory as one way of answering the question, "How can a complex collaboration between components evolve in small steps?" Notice that this is precisely the question that Intelligent Design tries to short-circuit by saying that only God could have done it.

As a metaphorical vignette standing for the whole theory, Cairns-Smith offers the memorable image of "an arch of stones" (complete with a drawing of a little arch made of ten stones). This "might seem to be a paradoxical structure if you had been told that it arose from a succession of small modifications, that it had been built one stone at a time. How can you build any kind of arch *gradually*? The answer is with a supporting scaffolding." In this case, you'd pile up a rounded heap of stones to act as scaffolding and then lay the arch down, one stone at a time, on top of it, and "then you would remove stones to leave the 'paradoxical' structure." In this image, the arch is DNA-based life, and the metabolic processes that Cairns-Smith postulates as having developed in clay are the scaffolding that falls away after the arch is complete.

And by the way, the word *claymation* is a linguistic example of a related process: it derives from the word *animation* (meaning the process of bringing to life) but along the way the root of the word — *anima*, meaning life — has fallen away, leaving us with something that refers to *lifelike* clay without any mark in the word itself of how it got that way.

But what caught my attention here is that a *cairn* is in fact "a rounded or conical heap of stones erected as a memorial or landmark" and a *smith* is "one who constructs, builds or produces something," so a *cairns-smith* is someone who constructs memorial heaps of stones. This is the little discovery that I want to think about in the remainder of this section.

After finding that Cairns-Smith was alive, I emailed him to ask if he'd thought of this, or if anyone else had ever pointed it out. He emailed back to say no, but he thought it was very clever. I don't know if he meant that *clever* sarcastically.

At first it surprised me that nobody seems to have noticed. But when you think about it, who would be likely to notice such a thing? It would have to be someone who reads and thinks about both science and poetry (that would be me); somebody attuned to self-referentiality, metaphor and wordplay in scientific discourse (me again), most likely someone trained in deconstruction (me); probably an American for whom the name Cairns-Smith stands out as particularly quaint or curious (again me). And is it any wonder that this bit of self-referentiality — in a theory of how clay became alive — should be noticed by someone whose own name happened to be "Living Stone"?

Does this mean I'm not necessarily so clever, just well-positioned? That for the very un-mysterious reasons given, I'm simply the most likely person on the planet to have made this little discovery? That, if there were other people in my shoes, they probably would have thought of this too? Of course my own humility may have led me to discount the possibility that I may still be the greatest genius the world has ever known. If so, isn't it a shame that I've wasted my prodigious powers on little exercises like this?

In any case, it also seems likely that some kind of *overdetermination* (that is, a convergence of multiple factors) led Cairns-Smith to generate the image in the first place, working as he must have been both to articulate his theory and to leave a mark, to be remembered. The image serves at least the double purpose of illustrating the theory and of leaving a memorial to its author, but also in so doing to mark the immemoriality and authorlessness of the origins of life in the first place. It is very important to notice that its multiple paradoxical reflexivities make this more than just an additive network of factors that increase the resonance of this particular image. They make it more like an organism! We recognize this in common parlance by the way a seemingly casual metaphor *takes on a life of its own*. This points the way to the serious question of whether language can be considered to be *alive*.

In the simplest terms, one could say that Cairns-Smith unconsciously left a signature: theory as autobiography. I like to think of this through another image: while Daddy the Scientist was busy examining an important rock formation, with his magnifying glass, he didn't notice his child scratching the family name onto the other side. Professor Lee might have attributed the result to what Winnicot identified as two conflicting psychological principles: "the urgent need to communicate" and to be recognized, "and the still more urgent need not to be found."

But whatever individual psychological forces may be at work, these must also resonate with larger discursive forces. This kind of fractal resonance or linkage of small with large-scale dynamics, contributes to the overdetermination that produces the image. In this case, what seems to be operating is some permutation of a principle that French philosopher Michel Foucault famously called the *author function*. To make a long story short, in the premodern West, a kind of scientific authority was conferred by use of the great author's name ("Hippocrates says X"), while stories and poetry were valued as collective possessions that circulated anonymously, often orally. Modern science and literature emerge along with a reversal of this polarity. Literature comes to be valued by the name of the great author, while scientific validity attaches only to results that can be replicated by anyone. Falling back into pseudo-psychoanalytic terms, one might say that Cairns-Smith's signature constitutes a return of the repressed, the name of the author sneaking back right at the heart of this scientific theory, at the place where by metaphor it remains hinged to its literary other.

In any case, this signature, this artifact, qualifies as a kind of frozen accident (at least in Morowitz's sense of arbitrary noise made into meaning); it certainly makes for a paradoxical structure. We can say at least that it *performs*, via Cairns-Smith's text, that which the text seems to be about. I believe Cairns-Smith, that he had been unaware of it until I pointed it out: I see no reason for him to misrepresent this. So is it then the mark of a poetic intelligence attributable to his unconscious, or is it only the artifact of my own cleverness as a deconstructive close reader? Notice that this is not to ask "is it really there?" In either case, what it actually *does* is to take the proper name *Cairns-Smith*, something arbitrary and underdetermined, and make it meaningful by making it into a common noun, by linking it up and looping it back into a growing self-referential system.

The key concept here is "looping it back" — as genes emerge from and are looped back into metabolisms. This description of the verbal process that produced the artifact sounds uncannily like accounts of the emergence of metabolism by the yoking-together of chemicals into autocatalytic loops. Does this uncanny resonance mean that the intelligence that produced this verbal artifact is linked to some kind of primordial intelligence to be found in clay metabolisms, or simply that theories tend performatively to enact what would otherwise be merely their referential content? Or if all of this is an artifact not so much found as created by my own desire for meaning, is the desire really mine? Where, at what level, are we to locate desire, meaning, and intelligence? It is not that I favor a single answer to this question. I ask it because I am driven — if I wanted to speak more like a scientist, I would say *driven by my evidence* — to a multiple answer.

On the other hand, I could simply say that I am drawn just to the edge of where I can feel the ground slipping out from under my epistemological feet.

William Burroughs defined panic as "the sudden awareness that everything is alive and significant" — a kind of pantheism and animism. Only people who are seriously depressed talk about a "search for meaning"; what they are suffering from is how well-defended they are against the anxiety or mania of *too much* meaning. There is a more basic issue. We suffer not from a scarcity of meaning or some kind of existential aloneness in our intelligence but from an economy of overwhelming excess. To put it in cybernetic terms, the constitutive problem for systems is information control, to avoid being overloaded. Scientific reductionism and Intelligent Design are circuit-breakers. This is one of the reasons that science and religion can be so comforting.

Chapter Three

Getting Stuck and Unstuck

I. The Lamb Soup of Xinjiang

As you're reading this—and feeling variously inspired, amused, bored, or confused — could these very sentences — even this one you're reading right now, this annoyingly long sentence with its excessive clauses, dashes and commas — be sneaking into your brain and making subtle adjustments, like some kind of ninja chiropractor, so that, after a while, you start feeling limber, lighter, and the world seems to be opening up to you somehow, and you don't even know what it was that changed or what changed it?

Or is what you get out of your encounter with this (or any other) book limited in advance by what you want coming into it? If you're ardently seeking enlightenment, you might well find it here. In that case, though, you might find it anywhere. Just look at the way the light is playing on that bedspread!

Otherwise, if what you wanted was just a bit of engaging diversion, then how could the skies open up for you?

Or could you be drawn along by a glimmer of something beyond what you had originally wanted? As you were getting the snack you wanted, might it make you hungry for something more substantial?

Sometimes when I'm getting hungry and try to think of what I might want, a fleeting taste lights up some obscure web of neurons in my brain for a moment, like a breeze passing over a field, and my mind reaches for it: is it curry? Chile? Iona's lentil soup? The *molé* we had in Oaxaca? The lamb soup of Xinjiang?

But it's gone, and then I think, maybe it's not savory but sweet — and just then, something sweet flutters by — cake? Was it German chocolate cake? The cake from the Dominican place on the corner? My grandmother's *kugelhopf*?

As Thoreau put it,

> I long ago lost a hound, a bay horse, and a turtle-dove, and am still on their trail. Many are the travellers I have spoken to concerning them, describing their tracks and what calls they answered to. I have met one or two who have heard the hound, and the tramp of the horse, and even seen the dove disappear behind a cloud, and they seemed as anxious to recover them as if they had lost them themselves.

To rejoin with these mythical lost companions, whatever they may symbolize, would seem to make the world whole again. Freud traced this longing—and the sense of the nearness of its object, the sense of being on the verge of recovering a lost connection with all things, the experience of what he called *oceanic feeling* or what anthropologists used to call *mystical participation* — to infancy, nursing, being cradled in a mother's arms, not yet even conscious of oneself as a self, or farther back still, to the womb.

But notice that Thoreau's image is much more than a wish for sublime undifferentiation. To rejoin with the three mythical creatures would be again to become part of some primal plurality. It is not *oneness* but *someness*, like that embodied in Ezekiel's mystical vision of four living creatures — also, as it happens, like Thoreau and his lost companions, a human and three animals. And likewise the example that sprung to my mind, the lamb soup of Xinjiang. To someone like me, a Waspy Jew from Minnesota, it must represent *not* home, *not* mom, but something more like *diasporic belonging*, or if you like paradoxes, of being at home with radical difference. It is strange and familiar, strangely familiar and familiarly strange, comforting and exciting, quenching and sparking desire.

Did you sense it for a moment? Just a little? Even so, the moment recedes and the glimmer fades away. But please keep in mind as you read what follows: it's good that it fades away, or that sometimes it withdraws and hovers nearby, and sometimes it seems that it has been irrevocably lost. Home is never home as much as when you've gone away and come back, often repeatedly, the farther the better, or when you find it or make it somewhere far away. The most satisfying realization — so miraculous and liberating — is one that you must forget again and again in order to rediscover.

What is wanted is somehow to cultivate the continual approach to this state, to be continually in a state of approaching it, to be turned towards it. This is the stance cultivated in this book; not an embrace or an inhabitation of mysticism — but a turning-towards, a sustained approach, an entrance *Into the Mystic*.

II. Renunciation

As a curiously related example, think of the poet John Keats, whose characteristic stance came to be not one of approach but of poignant departure.

I think of him, in September 1820, dying slowly of tuberculosis, as he had already watched his mother and brother do, and on a ship about to leave England for Italy, where he already knew he would die, sooner rather than later, and thinking of his beloved Fanny Brawne, whom he is leaving behind, knowing he will never see her again, and writing of "the sense of darkness coming over me—I eternally see her figure eternally vanishing." I get a kind of visual image of these multiple departures within departures; a kind of continual, fractal, telescoping reverse zoom. If you can imagine how it's possible to have a continual moment of departure, while somehow all the moments of arrival and of being together have been factored out of the equation, then you'll understand what is meant by a *stance*. But the paradox of a continual departure has to remain unresolved. To resolve it by making this stance into a kind of frozen position in space — a statue in the posture of bidding farewell — is to miss the main point. A stance is more like an ongoing event in time than a structure in space; a way of coming into (or out of) engagement.

Freud watched his infant grandson playing a game with a spool of string, gleefully and repeatedly throwing the spool away from him and uttering what Freud heard as the German word "Fort" ("gone"). Much less often the child would utter the word "da" ("here") as he pulled the spool back. Freud understood this as the child's way of mastering, through fantasy and play, the otherwise uncontrollable and traumatic departures of his mother. Paradoxically, the trauma is mastered — at least in some provisional and imperfect way — by being *repeated*, over and over, but with the infant in the active role of banishing rather the than passive role of being abandoned (otherwise known as the "you're fired / I quit" response).

Even more fundamentally, the mother's actual departures are mastered by being symbolized, formalized into the spatial opposition of *there/here* or the verbal opposition *fort/da* — which might not even be words at all but just two opposed sounds, the important point being that presence/absence is turned into a *formal* opposition. Symbolization functions to distance the shattering immediacy of the comings and goings of the mother, to put them at one remove. This distancing is at the heart of language itself, just as the utterance of a word for something, at least in referential language, indicates the absence of the thing itself. In this view, the stance of being-in-language is a bidding farewell, a renunciation of things in themselves, of the immediacy of one's own experiences. But don't worry, this is only half the story — the tragic view of language, as Professor Lee put it — and we'll be turning to the other half as we go.

And by the way, among Keats's last words is the famous closing of his last letter to a friend: "I can scarcely bid you good-bye, even in a letter. I always made an awkward bow."

I think of a cinematic moment in a dream I had long ago that became for me a kind of mythic point of reference. In the dream I am driving, looking forward, but in the rearview mirror I can see that the city is on fire, buildings and bridges are collapsing, and even the road behind me is crumbling in some widening catastrophe that I manage to outrun only by moving relentlessly forward. As I came to understand this image, the "widening catastrophe" is, to start with, the tragic lives of my parents. The image took on a new dimension after 9/11/01, after having watched, from across the river in Brooklyn, the twin towers of the World Trade Center billowing black smoke and collapsing, and then collapsing over and over and over and over on television, being made into a defining moment that politicians would mobilize for all the fear and outrage attached to it. At some point it hooked up with my own personal narrative, where it seemed to me that my mother and father were like the twin towers, collapsing behind me. This is also what I mean by a *stance*— whether by trauma, by the bleakness of the present, but also in joy — being turned, turning one's being perpetually *toward the future,* while "at my back I always hear / time's winged chariot hurrying near."

As another counter-example, think of Walter Benjamin's famous Angel of History, hovering in mid-air, turned *away* from the future: "Where *we* see the appearance of a chain of events, *he* sees one single catastrophe, which unceasingly piles rubble on top of rubble and hurls it before his feet." The piles of rubble are the countless lost lives, even whole cultures and species come to naught, but above all, the countless betrayed revolutions, the attempts to establish paradise on earth, all failed and fallen short. The angel "would like to pause for a moment," Benjamin continues, "and to piece together what has been smashed. But a storm is blowing from Paradise" (that is, out of the Eden from which we were banished long ago), "it has caught itself up in his wings and is so strong that the Angel can no longer close them. The storm drives him irresistibly into the future, to which his back is turned, while the rubble-heap before him grows sky-high." The storm is "that which we call progress."

Facing the past, held aloft and unable to reorient himself, while falling backwards into an unknown future: this is the predicament of the Angel of History. Notice again, as in Keats' letter and in my own little story, the uncanny repetition: "unceasingly piles rubble on top of rubble"; "collapsing over and over and over"; "eternally see her figure eternally vanishing." These images give the sense of trauma and of involuntary flashback, of being frozen in place, eyes open, watching, mesmerized, horrified but unable to turn away.

III. Nonlinear Time Is Rife With Messiahs

Fortunately, the linear, progressive time in which the Angel of History is stuck isn't the only kind of time. What Benjamin calls *the now* (as distinguished from *the present* understood as a point in linear time) is "shot through with shards of Messianic time."

Since the sciences and social sciences have been so committed to linear time, other kinds of time have been relegated to science fiction. And partly because the way we have been taught to think about cause and effect — and about power and agency — have been so straight-jacketed and strapped to linear time, nonlinear time is rife with messiahs.

Before turning to the messianic, let's look in the other direction for a moment: at blockages in linearity that can be seen as such from a nonlinear perspective. In the large sense, when people understand the consequences of their actions at one remove but not two or three, the rest can seem mystical. The notion of *karma* is often invoked — where the consequences of one's own actions rebound to keep one stuck in a repetitive cycle, or as it is sometimes said, "what goes around comes around."

This is literally the case in gridlocked traffic. If you push out into the intersection on the yellow light and get caught there when it turns red, the drivers on the perpendicular street can't cross, and when you think of the ripple effect behind you both, being propagated not just straight behind you but around the block, you can see that it's as if you are the knot in a loop, in a whole knotted-up net. In other words, though you may not have realized, you are blocking *yourself*.

I remember walking in my neighborhood in Brooklyn and approaching a corner while walking alongside another pedestrian. A guy in a pickup had just stopped at the stop sign a moment before we arrived at the curb. The guy waited just long enough (only a second, in any case) for me and the other pedestrian to step off the curb — and then honked his horn just before we stepped in front of him. I saw the intense irritation on his face and realized immediately that he didn't understand that his hesitation was just long enough — by New York standards, anyway — to function as an invitation for the pedestrians to go first. By hesitating, he had put the potential obstacle in his own path! And by the way, not understanding how you put obstacles in your own path and then getting deeply frustrated about it is a great recipe for assorted health problems.

I once brought an old Minnesotan friend to Katz's Deli in New York, where you wait in one of several lines for the meat-carvers behind the tall counter to make your sandwich. We were in different lines, and when my friend finally joined me at the table, he was fuming. He complained that the guy behind the counter hadn't wanted to serve him. From the way he described it, I could guess how the stalemate he described had come to pass: he was waiting for the guy to turn to him and say *can I help you* (as they generally do in Minnesota) and the guy was waiting for him to just blurt out what he wanted (as we generally do in New York).

When he didn't, I can just hear the guy behind the counter thinking, *what's he waiting for, an engraved invitation?* Then, almost immediately (at least by Minnesota standards), the guy served the next customer. By the way, not understanding how you put obstacles in your own path, getting deeply frustrated about it — *and eating large pastrami sandwiches* — is an even better recipe for assorted health problems.

These are the simplest kinds of examples, almost as schematic as Edwin Abbot's famous 1884 novella *Flatland: A Romance of Many Dimensions*. In this satire, those who inhabit the two-dimensional surface of a plane view a visitor from the three-dimensional world as a mysterious and godly creature. For example, if limited to two dimensions, a square drawn inside a circle is stuck with absolutely no way out, not realizing that if a third dimension is available, the square could just step right out, just as we would step out of a circle painted on the floor.

This is not to say that we can think ourselves out of any lower-dimensional dilemma. But it does bring us to the messianic part.

Paul Atreides, hero of the 1965 classic sci-fi novel *Dune*, in a drug-enabled vision, sees time open up from a uniformly smooth flow into a "time nexus"; a turbulent "boiling of possibilities." The turbulence seems to derive from multiple feedback loops, especially the way Paul's own vision of what may happen and his possible resulting actions feed back into what may happen. Accordingly, the vision "incorporated the limits of what it revealed — at once a source of accuracy and meaningful error. A kind of Heisenberg indeterminacy intervened: the expenditure of energy that revealed what he saw, changed what he saw." This makes it seem as if the only agency and freedom — the only leverage that can be gained on an otherwise completely predetermined world — lay in *one's own* knowledge and actions. Or to put it another way, it seems as if one might know everything — that everything is predictable — except for oneself, one's own sovereign unpredictability.

But super-sized power is not the same as free will. Far from being a free agent, Paul Atreides is the product of generations of both genetic and cultural engineering by the women's secret society known as the Bene Gesserit, and he continues to be tormented by the cosmic carnage that his actions, squirm though he might, seem fated to generate: "somewhere ahead of him on this path, the fanatic hordes cut their gory path across the universe in his name."

Like Paul Atreides, Neo in the 1999 film *The Matrix* tries repeatedly to deny his fate only to find himself repeatedly fulfilling what has been prophesized for him. Even as the messianic figure known as The One, Neo is not unique but merely the latest incarnation of a structural contradiction in the system that periodically causes it to crash and to be rebuilt.

Again, notice that the hero's great power and its cosmic repercussions are beyond doubt, even though his freedom is called radically into question.

This grandiosity and paranoia — or at least, this extreme anxiety — involves the sense that one's every move might change everything, save the world, or destroy it, or somehow both. This stance is in dynamic tension with its opposite: depression, the sense that nothing one might do could make any difference at all.

IV. Depressive Realism

Depressed people have been shown to outperform non-depressed people in certain psychology experiments. In these experiments, subjects are given a set of shapes or numbers or game pieces and asked to predict whether these could be manipulated to yield a certain result according to certain rules. It turns out that non-depressed people tend to *over*estimate the likelihood that the desired result could be obtained. The more accurate view, according to these experiments, has been dubbed *depressive realism*. There's a lot of disagreement over what this phenomenon means or even whether it exists at all.

Without knowing the specific parameters of the experiments, it's a revealing exercise to try to think through how such an experiment would have to be set up. In particular, the situations would have to be of some mid-range complexity so that the likelihood of obtaining the result could only be more-or-less intuitively glimpsed. That is, it should neither be so transparent that the answer is obvious nor so opaque as to require a random guess. One kind of set-up that might fit these parameters, for example, would be the question of whether a given set of puzzle-pieces (not too large or small a set) could be arranged to yield a given shape. Even so, subjects could not be allowed to propose the use of a saw and hammer, since the possibility of altering the parameters at will would seem to favor non-depressed people more likely to act on a belief that "where there's a will, there's a way."

In other words, the situation has to be set up so that the belief of the subject as to whether the desired result is possible — or the desire of the subject for a result — can have no impact on whether the result is actually possible. But — and here's the kicker — such a set-up *favors depressives virtually by definition,* since depressives, sometimes described as suffering from "learned helplessness," tend to feel that nothing they do can alter the chances of desired results being obtained.

On the other hand, if the desire for an outcome (or if acting *as if* it were possible) can affect the possibility of that outcome being produced, we can speak of the *non-linearity* of the situation.

What kinds of situations are like this, and to what extent is our world non-linear in this way?

If I were to develop the conviction that I could become a professional basketball player (at age 55 and height 5′6″), you would be justified in calling me delusional. But what if I had developed such a conviction as a child, and my parents had shared the conviction? The chances would still have been vanishingly slim, though even in the past twenty years there *have* been a few pro basketball players as short or shorter than me. One thing, anyway, is obvious: my chances would have been non-existent *without* the conviction, however delusional. Even if I began to pursue this crazy ambition late in life, and even in the face of certain failure, it's still possible that I could positively transform my life in the process, and maybe squeeze a best-selling book and a movie deal out of it. (Critics are calling *My Crazy Ambition* "whimsical and quixotic, a moving testament to the strength of the human spirit.")

In this case, the desire would not affect the result in a straight-forward way — that is, the desire for x would not simply produce x. Instead, desires and processes and results would shape each other in a non-linear system with multiple feedback loops.

Recognize this? It seems we've stumbled back from the hypothetical into our actual world.

V. Theory of Mind

At first the happenings confused him. Then, as most of us would, he formed a mental model to reconcile the events with the way he believed the world behaves. The theory he came up with, however, was unlike anything most of us would devise: he was the subject of an elaborate secret scientific experiment. He believed the experiment was staged by a large group of conspirators led by the famous psychologist B.F. Skinner. (Leonard Mlodinow)

Just as infants must develop their own sense of self, they must also develop a notion of the separateness of others. This includes the realization that every person has a mind that is different from other minds and from one's own. We aren't born knowing this. It's something we have to learn, as has been demonstrated clini-cally by various experiments.

In the most famous of these experiments, the researcher plays a little game with the child, pretending that two dolls hide an object in a dollhouse — for example, a marble in a dresser drawer. Then, when one of the dolls is out of the house, the other doll removes the marble from the drawer and hides it again under a bed. When the first doll returns, where will she look for the marble?

Young children simply cannot grasp that the one doll — who was out of the house when the marble was moved — would still believe the marble is in the dresser. It is generally between ages three and four that a child will come to understand this. Such a child — realizing that the onlookers, along with the second doll, would know something that the first doll could not — is said to have developed a "theory of mind."

Notice that the notion that children develop their own theories of mind is really a theory of theory of mind, a meta-theory. It's called a theory in the first place since it is a hypothesis about the world that is not immediately obvious but is inferred from observation and then used as a principle to guide further interactions with the world. Calling it a theory recognizes that it is the product of mental operations, not simply a fact about the world.

You might be inclined to say, "isn't it obvious that people have their own minds? This is not a theory but a simple fact." Rather than get into the vexed and looping relationships between theories and facts, a few questions will serve to indicate the extent to which mind is really a theory. After all, what is the mind, anyway, and what is its relationship to the brain? Are the two distinguishable at all? Is the mind really a little model of the world, like a dollhouse? And to what extent is one's mind really one's own?

In a slightly different register, Freud described children as theorists about sexuality. Fed by various hints and clues but often thwarted in pursuit of answers, children are driven to theorize, sometimes revising their theories as new data is encountered — though, as scientists know, it is often easier to make the facts fit the theory.

I remember when, as a young child — I have no idea how old I was — I began to reflect on sexual difference. Spurred on (no doubt) by some fascinating new clue, I remember theorizing that women must have an orifice of some kind — some different kind of organ into which mine would fit. I remember that this notion seemed to me surreal, preposterous. It couldn't be! But, as Sherlock Holmes said, "when you have excluded the impossible, whatever remains, however improbable, must be the truth." Anyway, I kept it as an open question for further research. Sexual difference has always retained this exoticism for me.

Even beyond the sexual, of course, theorizing is what kids do continually, making observations and coming to conclusions, reality testing. Whatever else we do, we are theorists in a primary sense and from infancy. It is one of our original and ongoingly most important occupations. If anyone tries to tell you that being a theorist is a self-indulgent occupation for ivory-tower academics, please remind them of this. Theory is a way of life. Or to take it a step further, it makes a lot of sense to talk about life itself — collective life in its evolutionary trajectory in time and space — as a kind of theorizing and experimenting.

In the more classical version, theory involves a "world picture"; a little working model one keeps in one's head, and "reality checking" involves adjusting the model to make it correspond better to the real thing. The problem with this version is that the model is also *part of the real thing it models* — a part *of* it, not apart *from* it. How can you correspond to something of which you are a part? Holographs notwithstanding, you can't. The poverty of the "world picture" theory of theory is nicely illustrated by what is sometimes said about particularly otherworldly types: that they seem to have very carefully studied the manual of how to behave like a human being. The point, of course, is that without continuous feedback loops *between* world and image, each is radically estranged, but with the loops intact, they cannot be categorically distinguished. ᶜʰᵗ ⁱⁿ ᶜᵒˣⁱ ⁱⁿ ᵃᵗᵉⁿ

And there are other problems. The theorist questions things that others take for granted. Why? Generally, not out of pure pursuit of knowledge (as I mentioned earlier) but because the things are problematic or difficult for the person in question. If something comes easy to me, if I feel I know everything I need to know in order to do something well and I am fully satisfied, what would motivate me to theorize? I am more likely to want to leave well enough alone. Theorizing comes from conflict, lack, difficulty, desire. Not a disinterested explanation of things as they really are, but from interest, from a drive to participate in things, to intervene, to change and be changed by them: this is more like what can be called *love*.

To get deeper and deeper into theorizing, to theorize about more and more fundamental things, is to make more and more things difficult, in some sense to know less and less over time. My experience corroborates this observation. The more I develop as a theorist, the more I can see myself sitting in a chair thinking about whether to stand up and go to work, or answer the phone, or swallow, or blink, or go on thinking, or — actually, a grilled cheese sandwich would be pretty good right about now.

And by the way, the acquisition of theory of mind also means that telling lies is a developmental achievement, since it requires the understanding that people have particular knowledges and perspectives and thus cannot know or verify certain things. I remember when my friend's three-year-old started saying "mommy said" as a way of trying to get what she wanted (as in, "mommy said I can have a cookie"). This would seem to indicate she understood that others could not know, at that moment, whether mommy had said so or not, and thus that she had acquired theory of mind. But this example also indicates why we have to be careful about such inferences: it is also possible that she could have learned that the phrase "mommy said" was sometimes effective (for example, on some occasion where she had invoked it truthfully), and she was simply invoking it by rote, much as one learns that saying "please" can help to produce the result one desires.

Although many interactions look like communication, it is a very long way (for example) from (1) crying in frustration because I feel hungry and nobody is feeding me, to (2) understanding that others may not be able to figure out how I feel unless I tell them (something many adults have not fully grasped). Even if I cry on purpose because I want to be fed, it may be a simple reflex. I may not understand anything at all about the existence of others; I may have simply learned that when I cry I am more likely to get fed.

Interestingly, then, our own theory of mind is one of the things that makes it most difficult to assess whether a child (or some other creature) might really be employing some kind of theory of mind of their own. We are biased by our tendency to over-attribute mind — that is, consciousness and intentionality — to others. But it's at least one more twist more complicated than this, because part of how we help bring about the development of consciousness in infants is by *over-attributing* mind to them. Well before they could possibly understand language, we speak to them as if they might understand, and then by the way that we selectively respond to their responses, they begin to learn what we had attributed to them all along. This is why Professor Lee called the tendency to attribute subjectivity to things *love*. It has futurity and possibility in it; it both finds and invents the other, or in the words of the Chinese proverb, *dian shi cheng jin*: "point at a stone and it becomes gold." On the other hand, depressive realism might recognize that the infant was not capable of understanding language and think, "what's the point in talking to the baby? It can't understand anyway." Notice that, to a disastrous extent, this would also tend to be a self-fulfilling prophecy.

I cannot resist mentioning the 1996 research into "the animism of everyday life" in which researchers found that people routinely seemed to attribute subjectivity to objects, "giving them names, speaking to them, acting nonverbally toward them, and holding them to conventions of social reciprocity (feeling cheated by them, or guilty about abandoning them)." Subsequent research revealed that precisely 27.9 percent also made faces at their food. Thank god for sociology!

The tendency to grant subjectivity to things is what designers of computer-human interfaces count on being able to trigger. I often find that this gets in the way of the interaction since it requires an *extra* level of complexity from me: instead of simply treating the computer as another subject with whom I am inter-acting, I think something more like "*they* want me to treat the computer as a subject." This gets famously annoying when talking paperclips appear on screen to say, "it looks like you're writing a letter. Do you want me to help you?" (to which the obvious answer is, "just bugger off and leave me alone!").

When I play gin rummy on my computer and the program wins a hand, it displays the cards with the message "opponent has gin." Of course it means "*your* opponent has gin," as if the computer program were putting itself in my shoes by referring to itself as my opponent. It feels wrong to me, like I'm being deceived, and a little red flag goes up in my brain. I want to say: you don't *really* attribute agency to me! I think I'd have no problem if the program displayed instead the message "program has gin." Even "I have gin" would be better, though the assertion of subjectivity on the part of the computer is obviously faked. I can only surmise that the third person version and even the first person version are preferable because I am particularly on guard against *false empathy*.

One evening, Iona was explaining to me how she set her mobile phone to turn off automatically at a certain time every evening and to turn on again every morning. I asked some question about it, and she added, defensively, that she was only telling me for information's sake. This confused me, so I asked why she said it, but my question seemed to confuse her in turn, so I tried rather laboriously to spell it out: what were you thinking that I was thinking that you were trying to do if not give information? She said the tone of my response made her think that I thought that she was trying to tell me that *I should do it her way*. You can see the multiple orders of "mind-reading" at work here. And now I have to try to *read my own mind* since, though it had not occurred to me consciously that she was pushing on me her own way of doing things, maybe I had registered that at some level, and the tone of my voice really was pushing back. And maybe she believed that she wasn't telling me what to do, even though at some other level she really was posing her own practice as exemplary.

To put all this in more abstract terms: I recognize that you have some notion of me that is not the equivalent of my own notion of myself (and that neither of these fully accounts for the "actual" me, whatever that may be). I also know that you know that I am aware that your idea of me is not the same as my own, and I can see that this is why you might be able to say something like, "I know you think I'm just projecting onto you my own idea of who you are" (and if you do think so, you're right, since I don't think you know me at all). Beyond this, things begin to get a bit muddled for me (but maybe you're smarter than me and can sustain more levels of intentionality); the whole house of cards begins to collapse. I can write out the following words, but it's hard for me to wrap my mind around them: I know that you know that I know that you know that I'm aware of your idea of me.

When we go back to the first levels of this house-of-cards, we find that it was unstable to begin with. For example, I know that I am hyper-aware of false empathy, and of the difference between your idea of me and me, because I grew up with a mentally ill mother who cast everyone as characters in her own personal mythology. These characters had a lot of power, mostly the power to hurt but also the power to save, so I grew up both with an exaggerated sense of my own power over and responsibility for others, but also with an exaggerated sensitivity to being negated by others and their projected fictions of me. So you tell me: am I a mythological character or not? This is just a slightly exaggerated version of a universal dilemma in which we want to matter to others not just on their own terms but because of who we really are. It's a dilemma because ultimately there's no way of separating the two.

In fact, the representational model — in which people have miniature versions of me (or of the world) in the dollhouse worlds of their brains — is really a marker of pathology. Things change when we shift the terms from knowledge, recognition and representation to *desire*, which is less about how things are separated from each other than how they are connected. For me anyway, it is much easier to understand orders of intentionality this way, as in the simple sequence below:

(1) *I want you*. This is what we can call first-order desire. It's hard to distinguish from aggression, at least insofar as there's no indication that I care what you feel, *I just want you*. And by the way, when I say I want you, I'm proposing this as a hypothetical case. This is how phenomenologists use the first person pronoun: it's a hypothetical subject. So it doesn't mean that I *really* want you, okay? But on the other hand, it doesn't mean that I *don't* want you; I may in fact want you quite desperately. In fact, are you free later?

(2) *I want you to want me*. This is second-order desire, the desire to be desired — very poignant. It could be that I want my first-order desire for you to be reciprocated, but I could also want you to want me even if I don't particularly want *you*. I suspect that the desire for fame is like this, but I don't suffer much from that affliction. If I did, this would be a very different book!

(3) *I want you to want me to want you*. In other words, I don't simply want you to want me, since such a desire for me wouldn't

necessarily recognize my own feelings: you might as well be some kind of stalker! So we go a step further: I also want you to desire my desire for you. To put this a bit more crudely, I don't want you to jump on me whenever you just want me, but I do want you to jump on me when you feel that way *and* get the feeling that I do too.

(4) *I want you to want me to want you to want me.* It gets harder to wrap my brain around such high-level propositions, even though I feel them to be in play. It's harder when they're put into abstract formulae, easier when they're more embodied. In conjunction with the first three, this one seems to mean something like: I want you to want not just my desire but also my desire for your desire. In other words, if I do care how you feel, I also want you to care that I care, since otherwise, it wouldn't matter to you if you were with someone who didn't care about your feelings. But I should probably mention that, even though this is the case, I *still* want you to jump on me whenever you feel that I want you and you happen to want me, regardless of whether you think I'm particularly tuned into your feelings or not. Is that clear?

Reciprocal love and desire involve all of these levels and more; we could call it desire and love to infinity. In some kind of intersubjective landscape, we could represent it as a soaring peak. And there are also spiraling abysses, black holes, places of mutually reinforcing negation. I've been there too. In fact, as you may know, the tallest peaks and the deepest valleys are generally found together.

Here again we also have to go back to the first level and see that things weren't so simple to begin with. How did there get to be an "I" and a "want" and a "you" to begin with?

VI. Entification

Without knowing how much or in what ways our non-linear world can bend to our desires, how sanguine should we be about our powers?

To put it melodramatically, in estimating our own powers, we struggle to stay somewhere in the middle of a wobbly seesaw, with maniacal and messianic godliness at one end and helpless depression at the other. But if the question of how to attribute power and agency is an inevitable part of the human condition, its charge varies dramatically across cultures and times. To put it less melodramatically, it's less of a truth question and more a question of what is sometimes called *attributive style*.

To attribute any sovereign power is always to generate the same unresolvable contradictions: Is my agency or my choice or my desire really mine? Or in apparently desiring and making choices, am I merely the tool of forces beyond my control? On the other hand, how many of the obstacles I have understood as external are really projections of my own limitations and blockages? How much ventriloquizing (or as we say in cultural theory, how much *othering*) have I done? And ultimately, how is even that which we might call *God* a grotesquely magnified shadow of our own powers?

Chinese emperors ruled by the Mandate of Heaven, which would seem to invest an emperor with divine power and authority. Westerners who believed their own societies were characterized by smooth gradations of power had long caricatured the Chinese system as a bipolar one with an omnipotent emperor at one end and seas of powerless, faceless, and expendable masses on the other. But this is a classic case of *othering*, where one attributes faults to others in order to disavow them in oneself. In fact, unlike the more brittle Western principle of the divine right of kings, the Mandate of Heaven could be withdrawn from unjust or incompetent rulers. Accordingly, if various factions or emergent constellations of forces conspired to topple an unjust emperor or even to bring down a dynasty, it could always be said that the Mandate had been withdrawn. So while the concept seems to remove authority-granting agency entirely from the hands of the governed and give it to "Heaven" instead, it also returns it to people collectively in their various earthly groupings. This notion of Heaven comes to seem less like a place far, far away and more like Blake's notion of a God who "only Acts and Is in existing beings or Men."

To put the question about power and agency another way, how much good could a single person do? How much damage?

One poster child for the vicissitudes of individual agency — or to put it another way, the biggest *schlemeil* of all times — might be the American chemist Thomas Midgley,

> who invented both leaded petrol and CFCs [chlorofluoro-carbons]. Though lauded during his time, he has come to be known as having "had more impact on the atmosphere than any other single organism in Earth history" and "the one human responsible for more deaths than any other in history" due to his inventions. He eventually contracted Polio and lead poisoning and was left disabled in his bed. This caused him to create an elaborate system of pulleys and ropes in order to lift himself from bed. He died at the age of fifty-five after being strangled by one of his pulleys, and it is notable for the fact that both his inventions, leaded petrol and his pulley operated bed, contributed to his death.

In his various musings and disquisitions on related topics, manic-depressive Romantic poet Samuel Coleridge swung from one attributive-style extreme to another. Coleridge first embraced associationism, the hypothesis that complex behaviors — including the illusion of individual agency — emerge from the interaction of myriad forces, but later he came to reject and ridicule this view:

> Yet according to this hypothesis the disquisition to which I

am at present soliciting the reader's attention, may be as truly said to be written by Saint Paul's church as by me: for it is the mere motion of my muscles and nerves; and these again are set in motion from external causes equally passive, which external causes stand themselves in inter-dependent connection with every thing that exists or has existed. Thus the whole universe co-operates to produce the minutest stroke of every letter, save only that I myself, and I alone, have nothing to do with it, but merely the causeless and effectless beholding of it when it is done. Yet scarcely can it be called a beholding; for it is neither an act nor an effect; but an impossible creation of a something-nothing out of its very contrary! Itis the mere quick-silver plating behind a looking-glass; and in this alone consists the poor worthless I!

One of the ways of displacing this axis of abjection and grandiosity is to think in more distributed and networked ways about agency and causality. Social theorists have been developing various systematic ways of doing this, including what is sometimes called *actor-network theory*.

Psychologist Michael White, one of the founders of narrative therapy, invented his own clinical form of actor-network theory. White became known for his studies of children who compulsively soil themselves, a condition known as *encopresis*. The condition had mostly been diagnosed as a pathological form of rebellion against an intrusive and overbearing parent, usually a mother. But, as it happened, White did not find this dynamic in any of the cases he encountered. Rather than asserting that the accepted diagnosis got the family dynamic wrong, White avoided that argument simply by calling his own cases "*pseudo-encopresis.*"

And rather than attempt to get the child to reclaim agency and control — as previous therapies had done with very limited

success — White encouraged all the family members systematically to *externalize* the problem. They started simply by talking
about how it was affecting them, as if it were something
altogether external. The problem could then be given a name —
most memorably in one instance, "Sneaky Poo" — and treated as
a more-or-less independent agent. Additional entities could also
be invented as helpers for the child. This method turned out to be
extremely effective.

But wait a minute! How could this strategy possibly work? It
would seem that, if a child is acting out various unconscious
conflicts or family-system dysfunctions, the first step to a
solution would have to involve getting the child to recognize
these as such and then to reclaim responsibility. It seems like
madness — I mean dissociative and schizo — to encourage the
child and family to externalize further. It seems like this would
aggravate and entrench the problem.

If it does seem crazy, it's probably because the legacy of
enlightenment, humanism and rationality — and the capitalist
ideology in which these came to evolve — tend overwhelmingly
to attribute agency to individuals (and certainly *not* to fictional
entities that are the embodiments of system dynamics). And by
the way, if you don't believe that capitalism has driven this
ideology, go to Rockefeller Center in New York City, look up at
the looming, phallic building, and then back down at the big
brass plaque with the words of John D. Rockefeller inscribed
there: "I believe in the supreme power of the individual." I bet
you do!

Anyway, note also that White did not contest the truth of the
commonly accepted encopresis diagnosis and attempt to replace
it with a different explanation. Instead, he deferred the truth
question entirely by inventing another entity, "pseudo-
encopresis," which allowed him to explore and describe the
phenomenon on its own terms — or more to the point, to gain a
hearing without first having to pick a fight with the other more

established and powerful participants in the conversation. In other words, his own strategy mirrored that which he recognized and took seriously in his young patients: he was driven to invent an entity that, regardless of its status as discovered or invented, ended up altering the dynamics of its milieu (their families in the case of his patients, psychology and its categories in his own case). One of his patients called his entity Sneaky Poo, and he called his Pseudo-Encopresis. Pretty sneaky, eh?

For now, all I want to say about this mirroring is that it's one of the signatures of complex systems. As you may have noticed, the mirroring extends outward: this complex system peopled with entities that are paradoxically both real and invented is not just the family, or psychology: it is our world. And whether we identify as "individuals" or otherwise, we are such entities ourselves.

Maybe even more surprisingly, those who study the origins of modern science tell a similar story. Early practitioners of what we now call science began to design experiments to control variables — and sometimes publicly to reenact their experiments as a kind of theater. Variables are rigorously controlled — that is, scientific method is practiced — so that, ideally — *only one* conclusion is possible — or as it is sometimes phrased, so that the evidence can speak for itself. This situates the scientist as the one who has learned to stand aside and let Nature speak in her own voice. At the same time, this was an ingenious way for an increasingly powerful non-aristocratic gentry and proto-middleclass to gain leverage on the world — to claim a kind of absolute authority — ventriloquized through the invented/discovered entity called Nature, and the practice that came to be called Science — without overtly contesting the aristocratic and religious authorities that otherwise had the world all nailed down between them. In other words, like Michael White and his encopresis patients, they invented entities (Nature and Science) that enabled them "to gain a hearing without first having to pick a fight with the other more established and powerful participants."

So is science too an invented entity, really a form of politics, a way of leveraging power and authority from one set of interests on behalf of others? Doesn't this compromise the objectivity of science and undermine the crispness of its distinction from other practices? Yes and no. Science is a participant in a complex social ecology, in a constellation of relationships with other discourses and ideologies (religion, politics, art, and so on) — as well as having to answer to what is sometimes called the material world (though of course the social and discursive networks are fully material as well). But if science were not a creature of this ecology, if it did not exist in a co-evolving relationship with these various other entities and their environments, it couldn't exist at all!

Most people seem to embrace the warm-and-fuzzy truism that the whole is greater than the sum of its parts, but if you really have the courage of your convictions, it's a challenging notion. If we're part of some collective entity — for example, a family or an institution or a nation or a planet — where exactly can we find the excess that exceeds each of us? Does the gigantic collective entity have something like a mind of its own, operating in some meta-dimension with other meta-entities, mostly beyond our direct control or knowledge? Even more disturbingly, at the small end (where we all live), does the excess also loop back and get reinserted, like "bugs" in the system that come back to haunt it, like animated characters in a live-action film, as if ghosts and other assorted entities were moving among us?

What if the names we gave these ghosts and gods and demons were *ghosts* and *gods* and *demons*?

VII. Famous Poems Made Up of One Enormous Word

Scientists who investigate emotion tend to identify several basic or primary emotions—usually about six of them, divided into positive and negative. They distinguish emotions from closely related phenomena such as feelings and moods, and primary from secondary or mixed emotions.

Psychologist Paul Ekman, one of the pioneers in the field, divides his book *Emotions Revealed* into chapters on sadness, anger, surprise and fear, disgust and contempt, along with what he groups together as the "enjoyable emotions." These seven, he says, are "experienced by all human beings" and "have clear universal expressions" on the face.

I'm not buying any of it.

When I consult my own experience (colored, admittedly, by my training in cultural theory), every single one of Ekman's points seems profoundly wrong. Of course there aren't precisely six emotions, or seven. And they are all complex and multi-layered and can't be divided unambiguously into positive and negative or pure and mixed. They can't be distinguished categorically from feelings or moods. And they aren't universal.

I want to say: I'm *surprised* at this kind of reductionism; it *saddens* me and makes me *angry*, and I have to admit to a certain amount of *contempt* — which of course I also *enjoy*, since the extent to which scientists are unable to give an even remotely adequate account of emotion leaves more room for the rest of us who think systematically about such things. I want to say, adapting a mean-spirited old witticism: a scientist studying emotion is like a dog walking on its hind legs. It's not that it's done well, but one is surprised to see it done at all.

To be fair, scientists are just getting started studying this sort of thing. I'm not talking here about psychoanalysts and thera-pists, who have been studying emotion through their own practices for more than a hundred years, but the guys in white lab coats, the ones who are committed to traditional scientific method, experiments and statistics.

Well, at least a start has been made, the scientists can say. Concepts and categories hard-edged enough to be tested and revised (they might say), *even if they are all wrong*, are an

improvement over impressionistic mush and untestable philosophical phantasmagoria. This is how science works. And
besides, isn't making fun of scientists who study emotion the
most reactionary kind of response? Cold rationality and hard
science moving into the neighborhood of the warm and fuzzy?
Harrumph!

To balance out the caricature of reductionist scientists, take an
example from what is arguably the extreme other end of the
spectrum.

Jorge Luis Borges's famous short story, "Tlön, Uqbar, Orbis
Tertius," is consummate postmodern fiction, in many ways the
opposite of science. It's the fictional story of a secret society that
invents a fictional planet called Tlon, which is imagined in turn
as having its own forms of fictional literature: a fiction of a fiction
of a fiction. In the languages of Tlon's northern hemisphere (the
narrator explains),

> the prime unit is not the verb, but the monosyllabic
> adjective. The noun is formed by an accumulation of adjec-
> tives. They do not say "moon," but rather "round airy-light
> on dark" or "pale-orange-of-the-sky," or any other such
> combination. In the example selected, the mass of adjec-
> tives refers to a real object, but this is purely fortuitous. The
> literature of this hemisphere . . . abounds in ideal objects,
> which are convoked and dissolved in a moment, according
> to poetic needs. At times they are determined by mere
> simultaneity. There are objects composed of two terms, one
> of visual and the other of auditory character: the color of
> the rising sun and the faraway cry of a bird. There are
> objects of many terms: the sun and the water on a
> swimmer's chest, the vague tremulous rose color we see
> with our eyes closed, the sensation of being carried along
> by a river and also by sleep. These second-degree objects
> can be combined with others; through the use of certain

abbreviations, the process is practically infinite. There are famous poems made up of one enormous word. This word forms a poetic object created by the author.

Note how diametrically this passage is opposed to all of what would characterize a scientific approach. Borges is concerned here with the realm of the poetic and aesthetic rather than the rational; with impressionistic and subjective experience rather than with the objective and consensual worlds of science. He is interested in what is fleeting rather than the solid and durable; in that which is irreducibly complex and comes in infinitely plural combinations rather than in the finite and numerable set of fundamental elements so dear to reductionist science.

In fact, it seems as if Ekman's and Borges's approaches were shaped by a mandate to be as unlike each other as possible, as if science and literature had evolved by differentiating themselves from each other. And this is pretty much what happened over the course of Western modernity, beginning in the Renaissance. Of course the spectrum has more than two ends; it is really an ecology of various interlocking niches and strategies. In Western modernity, art, science, religion, and politics are maximally differentiated from each other. You can tell by the extent to which a member of any of these categories is compromised by resemblance with any of the other areas. Religious science or scientific religion, political art or artistic politics (and so on) tend to be regarded as inferior if not as downright abominations, at least in the Modernist view.

So what would it mean to split the difference between Borges and Ekman, to aspire to be both and neither science and literature, and why not art and religion and politics too? No doubt it would mean first of all *to fail*. And places have already been made for such failures. Sometimes we call the rigorous ones *philosophy* or sometimes, simply, *essays* (which is to say, *attempts*). But what if our perversity were infinite; what if we aspired not just to be both and neither, but also were determined to avoid being relegated to whatever default categories may be reserved for the both-and-neither? What if we aspired to be all and none of the above?

This is the question that the essays in this book endeavor to keep open; it is precisely what is *essayed* or *assayed* here. Call it perversity of the most dogged kind, persevered perversity. It amounts to a kind of algorithm, a set of "rules of engagement," *a poetics*, which is to say, a way of making things: the desire to remain equidistant from literature and art, science, religion, politics, and the marketplace — or if you prefer, to participate equally at every moment in them all. And by the way, this is not some kind of maverick individualism. Quite the contrary: it seems to be a version of the principle by which computer animators reproduce the movements of flocks and herds, which in turn seems to be related to the principle by which actual flocks and herds move: creatures are driven to stay *close but not too close* to their fellow creatures.

I remember once when my granddaughter was about two years old, we were at a restaurant, and her father admonished her to use her spoon properly, to scoop up her food with the rounded end of the spoon and to transport it into her mouth. Then, quietly and without making much of a show of it, she proceeded to explore various ways of improper spoon use: sticking the handle of the spoon into her food, licking the back of the spoon, rubbing the spoon on the top of her head, dropping it on the floor (apparently by accident) and so on. Perversity — which here consists in doing everything but what one is enjoined to do — amounts to a sustained exploration of *possibility space* (here the human/spoon interface), and it seems to come as easily as water flowing in multiple directions around an obstacle. Some of this spirit informs the French term *bricolage,* used to refer to a kind of creativity that makes do with whatever is at hand, or the Hindi slang term *jugad,* which I've seen rendered into English as "work-around." In English, the word *play* just might say it all.

The spoon vignette works as a kind of antidote to Freud's story of his grandson and the *fort-da* game: the paradigm of play and perversity versus the paradigm of attempted mastery, tragedy and loss.

In fact, the modern ecology of discourses like science and literature — like other ecologies — does not thrive on absolute and rigid separations between realms (on purity, that is) but on controlled mixings and permutations and hierarchizations. Borges mixes the short story — in many ways the most literary genre of fiction — with that bastion of sober factuality, the encyclopedia. Ekman takes rationalist reductionism into realm of the subjective and impressionistic world of emotion (though perhaps to keep the warm-and-fuzzy from rubbing off on him, he exaggerates the macho reductionism). Both of these strategies represent permutations of the principle of permutation.

So we could say that science and art and politics and religion have carved up the world among them, through a dynamic process of ceding territory to the others in exchange for more-or-less exclusive rights to particular realms of their own, or by simply scavenging whatever was left after the stronger had its fill. But this way of saying it doesn't quite capture the dynamism of the process: the participants continually co-evolve as other creatures do, becoming who they are through the jockeying-for-position. To zig rather than zag is to become something else. And as the vast array of living creatures testify, there are lots of different strategies, lots of ways of succeeding. There's not just one game in which all compete, not one hierarchy.

Notice that this is not quite what is called a system with "no positive terms" — that is, a system in which the identities of the elements are exclusively their differences from other elements. But neither is it a system in which the identities of the elements are specified in advance and then evolve — and become knit together into a system — by coming into relation with other elements. These are the kinds of accounts of systems and their members you get when you're looking for their identities; their properties. But they can be seen in their aliveness only if you look instead for their capacities for engagement, the possibility spaces available to them, their vectors, their stances.

The identities of the participants — the *players* — are not given in advance but emerge and change as they go. The Tlönian poetic objects of Borges—"famous poems made up of one enormous word" — those reflexive, metafictional, sublime, fleeting, hyper-complex constellations of events and qualities that barely cohere into objects at all — turn out to have a fairly robust resemblance to actual discourses, personalities, living creatures, ecologies — ourselves.

So here we are again, back in our actual world!

Chapter Four

Beginning Again

I. Chaos and Complexity Theory

I would not give a fig for the simplicity this side of complexity, but I would give my life for the simplicity on the other side of complexity. (Oliver Wendell Holmes)

i accept chaos. I am not sure whether it accepts me. (Bob Dylan)

i. Learning to See Chaos

Like many non-scientists, I first learned about chaos theory — as it was widely called at the time — from James Gleick's 1987 popularization, *Chaos: The Making of a New Science*, which led me to mathematician Benoit Mandelbrot's classic 1977 *Fractal Geometry of Nature*.

I remember, shortly thereafter, standing on a beach in the flux of the waves. At my feet, the sinuous fingers of the sea sent smaller fingers of froth reaching up onto the sand, waves of waves, all webbed with networks of foam made up, in turn, of smaller networks of bubbles, webs of webs. Above me, cirrocumulus clouds sprawled across a blue sky, popcorn clusters of clusters and wisps of feathery wisps. Everything had become fractal, very roughly describable as pattern (often self-similar pattern, as in these cases) at multiple scales.

Learning to see chaos represented, for me, a kind of re-enchantment of the world. No doubt some version of this experience is widely shared by those in the throes of any old paradigm shift: the sense of being "present at the creation," the zeal of the convert. And in retrospect, gradual paradigm shifts can tend to seem more and more like acute conversion experiences. Even so, this episode of worldmaking bears some very specific historical resonances, even in my highly condensed and aestheticized version. What I saw happening to my world was stark modernist formalism being deconstructed into baroque, postmodern plenitude and excess. On a beach in Massachussetts.

Part of the conversion to chaos involves learning to see structures not as structures but as events in process, which is part of what makes chaos and complexity theory full partners with poststructuralist theory generally. Sociologist Niklas Luhmann describes society as a complex system whose basic elements are acts of communication; that is, "not stable units (like cells or atoms or individuals) but events that vanish as soon as they appear." Likewise (for example), when you deconstruct the image of a human body as a structure with a simple boundary between inside (self) and outside (nonself), you get something much more dynamic and fractal. Negotiations between self and nonself (and the continuous transformations of one into the other) happen not just at the skin but fractally and at multiple scales down to the cellular level: every cell in the body is engaged in this negotiation; in fact, every cell *is* this negotiation. If the body is a structure, it is a fractal one with all edges and no interior — a whirlpool, a burning bush.

(And by the way, as you were reading those words, did you feel your body subtly opening up, exquisitely flayed and aflame, and in the process, a new sense of being-in-the-moment? If so, you've already drunk the Koolaid and you can skip the rest of this section. Otherwise keep reading.)

These examples (of Luhmannian society and deconstructed bodies) are intimately related to poststructuralist accounts of texts not as hermetic interiors but as intertextual negotiations, and more generally to the concurrent paradigm shift in cybernetics from closed to open systems (about which, more in the next chapter).

On the scientific side, Prigogine and Stengers' 1984 *Order Out of Chaos* and Stuart Kauffman's 1993 *The Origins of Order: Self-Organization and Selection in Evolution* were influential in developing fully temporal accounts of chaos and complexity.

Under their influence, I remember walking in the Nevada desert and noticing some of the ways that the scarcity of water shapes the plants and their interactions. I saw it in the spacing of their branches and blossoms, the shapes of their leaves and stems, their own spacing in the terrain, all selected to optimize water absorption and retention. Looking at a sagebrush bush, I saw a living algorithm in multidimensional possibility space, its form-in-process an ongoing exploration of this space.

(A bit more metacommentary: so far these little autobiographical vignettes borrow from the romanticized image of the scientist in the "eureka" moment: "his hair was a ragged mane, . . . his eyes were sudden and passionate," etc. — that was Gleick's description of physicist Mitchell Feigenbaum. But let me see if I can go on to make it even a little more uncomfortable.)

The desert ecology felt deeply strange and deeply familiar to me. What I recognized in the sagebrush was a fellow creature engaged, like me, in the question of how to find what nourishes you in the middle of a desert. "Danger makes human beings intelligent" as Anna Freud put it. If this attitude strikes you as hopeless anthropomorphization or New Age twaddle, consider the following interchange:

> Chuang Tzu said, "See how the minnows come out and dart around where they please! That's what fish really enjoy!"
>
> Hui Tzu said, "You're not a fish—how do you know what fish enjoy?"
>
> Chuang Tzu said, "You're not I, so how do you know I don't know what fish enjoy?"

This, in any case, is also the kind of questioning, of both kinships and differences, that chaos and complexity make possible.

ii. Complexity

Complexity and chaos both have a range of technical definitions, but both remain nonetheless profoundly ambiguous and paradoxical.

The paradox of complexity can be indicated quickly: "if what we are interested in is complexity itself, then an image that we can easily identify as complex is thereby *less* complex than one whose complexity we find difficult or impossible to ascertain."

In the example of a social system as described by Luhmann, complexity derives from "an observer's inability to define completely all [the] elements' connections and interactions. . . . [T]here is no totalizing perspective or omniscient selector. Each act of observation is embedded in what it observes." Such a definition should also be historicized: only against the *fantasy* of a disinterested, totalizing and transcendently objective perspective—a fantasy most specific to imperialist modernity— can complexity come to be defined as embeddedness, or rather, as the contradiction between transcendence and embeddedness.

Physicist Stephen Wolfram's quick definition of complexity also coordinates an observed and an observer:

> In everyday language, when we say that something seems complex what we typically mean is that we have not managed to find any simple description of it—or at least of those features in which we happen to be interested.

This notion — of the impossibility of simple description — gestures toward a range of possible philosophical commitments, from antireductionism to extreme nominalism. Wolfram (no philosopher) seems to remain committed to an extreme reductionism in which complex behavior always derives from the iteration of simple rules. Even so, his Principle of Computational Equivalence suggests some of the more world-changing implications of complexity. Wolfram posits first "that all processes, whether they are produced by human effort or occur spontaneously in nature, can be viewed as computations," and second, that "almost all processes that are not obviously simple can be viewed as computations of equivalent sophistication." Recognizing a single common level of complexity (or *virtual kinship* as I have called it) radically undercuts the master narrative of growth and development as increasing complexity.

iii. Chaos

Nailing down chaos as a concept is also difficult, first of all, since even scientists use the word in several ways. Sometimes the word is used in its popular sense as a synonym for simple disorder. In this case, the more complex and fruitful kind of disorder — the kind of disorder out of which order can emerge — tends to be identified as "the *edge* of chaos." More often, though, *chaos* is used to mean the complex disorder itself, but to make things more confusing, it can also refer to the kind of order that *emerges* from such disorder. And here's the punchline: this ambiguity is not so much an obstacle to be cleared away but something more like *what chaos really is*.

The word comes from ancient Greek, where it signified the primal emptiness of space, the nothing from which something emerges. As it turns out, postmodern physics has elaborated this notion nicely: time and space are "crystallized from nothingness," and empty space, it turns out, "is not so empty — it is actually seething with activity" — the generative chaos of a "blooming, buzzing confusion" (as Victorian psychology pioneer William James famously described the perceptual world of the infant out of which, as the child learns to focus, discrete figures emerge). Physicist Frank Wilcek calls this non-empty emptiness the Grid. The Grid is reality's substrate, built from a host of ingredients: quantum commotion; the metric field that delineates space, time and gravity; exotic materials like the quark-antiquark condensate and the Higgs field that together transform empty space into a multilayered, multi-coloured semiconductor.

Ancient Greek cosmology, postmodern physics, Victorian psychology — why engage in a transhistorical treasure hunt for exemplars of chaos, like an old Jungian sniffing out archetypes? Well, first, because I want to offer examples that best give the feel of chaos, but also to gesture again at the questioning of kinships and differences chaos makes possible, this time by suggesting that it offers at least the possibility of tracing different constellations with past knowledges, rearranged genealogies and relationships between science and literature and religion. This is part of what I mean by *beginning again*.

iv. Cooking Up Complexity

Let me try to show you complexity stripped down to its most basic, or if you like paradoxes, simple complexity.

First step: start with several things and processes. It may seem obvious, but it's important to recognize that, whenever you have several things, it means that they *are not alike*, even if they are (for example) three hydrogen atoms. Multiplicity involves difference.

Thus physics begins with certain particles and forces; biology, with assorted chemicals and their various interactions; language, with letters and words and grammar. Notice that, while sciences may fetishize a countable set of basic elements ("simples" that cannot be divided any further), things start getting stickier when you try to nail them down. The more physics tries to identify a basic set of particles (for example), the more they seem to multiply and evaporate into probabilistic clouds. Again it seems that this difficulty is unavoidable: the discretely countable seems to emerge out of a more primal multiplicity; I've called it *someness*.

As in other recipes, after assembling the ingredients (nouns), you need to do something with them (verbs): *start combining them*. In order to generate chaos and complexity, the process of combination has to involve nonlinearity or *recursion* — the product of a process being fed back into the process again. But note that even simple mixing is describable as recursion.

Recursion in mathematics, where the result of a function is fed back as a starting value for the next iteration, is most famously illustrated by the Mandelbrot set, an infinitely complex fractal object generated by a very simple, repeatedly iterated equation.

Autocatalysis is an example of recursion in chemistry. In the simplest version, one of the products of a reaction catalyzed by some particular chemical is *more of the catalyst itself*, which thus continues to catalyze more of the reaction as long as more raw materials are present. In a modestly rich chemical environment, such reactions can develop complex self-amplifying and also self-inhibiting loops: behold the emergence of *metabolism!*

There is recursion in linguistics, starting with the way grammar enables the embedding of clauses in other clauses. This has been proposed as the way that grammar, given a finite series of elements, "can produce an infinite number of sentences of unbounded length" (as I fear the reader may think is a pretty good description of this book). Even if there might be languages that lack recursion at the grammatical level (a controversial point, at this writing), recursion is nonetheless "part of how all humans think — even when it is not part of the structure of their languages." Consciousness and language are recursive loops in an already very loopy universe.

There are also multiple forms of sociological recursion. Ian Hacking describes the process of social construction of identities as a nonlinear process of "Making Up People" in which (for example) a category like "autism" or "multiple personality disorder" co-evolves in tandem with a target group of people and with sets of social practices, institutions, specialists, and so on. The various components are bound together by a series of recursive loops and the whole configuration emerges, changes, grows, breaks apart, dissolves, and so on.

Discursive recursion is the subject of Andrew Abbott's *Chaos of Disciplines*. Taking sociology as his main example, Abbott shows how any particular division of the field, for example into quantitative and qualitative methodologies, only generates further fractal divisions: the qualitative side itself will turn out to have a quantitative and a qualitative side, and so on. When such divisions are engaged not just as structures but as processes (versions of what is known in mathematics as *binary decomposition*), one is likely to find complex cycles of disciplinary polarizations, hybridizations, and so on.

And there are several important kinds of recursion in literature. Structuralist linguist Roman Jakobson defined *poeticity* as that aspect of a message that refers back to itself. In the most basic sense, rhyme and meter and other devices self-referentially call attention to language as language rather than — referentially — to any content. And there are multiple ways that literature works recursively to thematize its own operations, starting with plays-within-plays, metafiction, and other self-referential maneuvers.

As a somewhat random example (or see my other books for a great many more), take Alice Walker's well-known 1973 short story "Everyday Use." The story is set in the 1960s; the narrator is a tough old African-American woman who lives in the rural South with her younger daughter Maggie. She is visited by her upwardly mobile older daughter, Dee (also known as Wangero), who is returning from a northern city where she has discovered Black Power and high culture, making her painfully condescending to her family of origin. Dee/Wangero asks for a family quilt to take back with her to display but, in a sudden and almost religious inspiration, the mother gives the quilt instead to her younger daughter, even though Maggie will only put it to "everyday use."

Even in this thumbnail account, it's easy to guess at least one way the story is looped back around self-referentially: the story itself is an artifact rather like the quilt, part of the cultural legacy of mothers to daughters. If you wanted to shut down interpretation, you could try reducing to a slogan the reinsertion of the story into itself: stories, like quilts, are best put to use rather than aesthetically revered as art. This reading will only do the trick if you're allergic to interpretation — and to chaos and complexity. Otherwise, finding the recursivity helps you open up a set of generative contradictions at the heart of the story, such as the vexed relationship between art and utility. Even the apparently simple proposition that short stories can be understood as utilitarian objects implies a radical redefinition of utility with paradigm-shifting consequences.

Again I want to stress the experiential aspect of engaging recursive chaos and complexity, here via the reading and writing of literature. The way that a piece of literature is about itself is something that one often discovers only belatedly; it does not short-circuit interpretation but begins it anew. Likewise, in listening to poetry, the recursivity of the language need not produce an alienating art-for-art's-sake closure but can instead increase the living-thing-likeness of the language, its excessive layers of mediation working to intensify the sense of immediacy of the experience. And the act of writing in the grip of recursion is not a navel-gazing exercise but a much more dynamic process, a surfing in the recursive curl of things. Find that moment and try to sustain your balance in it.

v. What It All Means

So what does it mean that we can find chaos and complexity in what is called nature and in the works of our own hands and brains, literature in particular, especially when we weren't exactly intending to place them there? I suggest three main ways of approaching this question.

First, it is often claimed that chaotic and complex processes are universal, so we should expect to find them everywhere — transculturally, transhistorically, and on both sides of the nature/culture divide.

For example, Oliver Sacks proposes that the often conspicuously fractal visual hallucinations experienced by many people who suffer from migraines derive from the fractal structures of the brain:

> these hallucinations reflect the minute anatomical organization, the cytoarchitecture, of the primary visual cortex, including its columnar structure — and the ways in which the activity of millions of nerve cells organizes itself to produce complex and ever-changing patterns. We can actually see, through such hallucinations, something of the dynamics of a large population of living nerve cells and, in particular, the role of what mathematicians term deterministic chaos in allowing complex patterns of activity to emerge throughout the visual cortex. This activity operates at a basic cellular level, far beneath the level of personal experience. They are archetypes, in a way, universals of human experience.

The paradoxes here are compelling: apparently it takes a hallucination — seeing something not really there — to see self-referentially what really *is* there, namely, the neurological mechanism *by which* we see. And the dazzling complexity of this vision, this ethereal meta-reflection, seems to derive from how it short-circuits us back to the solid substrate, the hardware. To put it another way, the universality of chaos and complexity loops back around to complicate and paradoxify even the simple assertion of their universality.

Of course, suspicion of universalized truth claims is also a leading operating principle of cultural theory. I'm still a card-carrying poststructuralist, which is why I will only identify this as a "leading operating principle" and not a truth claim itself (although the claim that "there are no universals" is at least interestingly contradictory). But it needs to be pointed out, too, that the *rejection* of universality claims often functions as a rear-guard action to bolster the nature/culture divide and to maintain the monopoly of humanists over the culture side. Although this maneuver may have some strategic value (for example, in trying to fend off scientists with their reductive explanations for everything), it's a rear-guard action insofar as it's driven by an exceptionalism about humans that is, as I have already argued, ultimately a *theological* position.

Universality is understood in chaos theory as the prevalence of certain mathematical processes over a range of otherwise disparate phenomena. As I have already indicated, such prevalence need not be understood as difference-effacing similarity but as a kind of *virtual kinship*, what I have also called *withness*: language resembles the world of which it is a part; it *bears withness* to its world. If you prefer to stress difference rather than resemblance, you can start by considering instead how the plurality of all that is called "language" is riven by differences as radical as those that cleave language from the world.

The charged question of universality aside, we can trace historically particular discursive forces at work whereby literature came to occupy a privileged position to engage chaos and complexity. In an emergent modern ecology of discourses in the West, coming to a head around 1800, recursion and self-reference were banished from science and became the particular province of what came to be called literature. Foucault's account is that literature emerged as

> merely a manifestation of a language which has no other law than that of affirming — in opposition to all other

forms of discourse — its own precipitous existence; and so there is nothing for it to do but to curve back in a perpetual return on itself; as if its discourse could have no other content but the expression of its own form.

We can trace this legacy in literature and literary studies over the past two hundred years, from Coleridge's principle of organic form, to Aestheticism's art for art's sake, to structuralist accounts of language-as-system, to Jakobsonian poeticity, to the insistence of the so-called New Critics (in the mid-twentieth century) that literary texts and literature in general be treated as self-contained systems, and into postmodernism's anti-realisms and metafictions. And what does it mean for literature and literary studies that science now has also begun to embrace recursion and self-reference? This remains an open question. The melancholy account is that literature, the novel, poetry (and so on) are well on their way to extinction, their niche in the modern discursive ecology having been invaded and compromised from all directions. On the contrary, it seems to me more like their modern incarnations are turning out to have been just a warm-up act — stay tuned!

Finally, the argument can also be made that paradigms of chaos and complexity are in some larger and primary sense historical constructions of postmodernity and late capitalism. This can be understood as an epistemological claim that our history shapes our understanding of the world and (for whatever reasons) is now causing us to notice and to name and to know chaos and complexity in new ways. A more ontological historicist claim can also be made: that chaos and complexity are actually being more intensively produced, selected for, in the present era. In this account, capitalist modernity is often understood as an epidemic of systematicizations — proliferating systems and subsystems — amid dynamic crosscurrents of trade and migrations and exchanges whereby "all that is solid melts into air."

But we can engage chaos historically without subscribing to linear historicisms, either the kind that traces a one-way trajectory of ever-increasing complexity, or the kind that finds a one-way determinism from economic base to ideological super-structure.

Chaos-and-literature pioneer N. Katherine Hayles rejects another (related) kind of linearity:

> In particular, I am not arguing that the science of chaos is the originary site from which chaotics emanates into the culture. Rather, both the literary and scientific manifesta-tions of chaotics are involved in feedback loops with the culture. They help to create the context that energizes the questions they ask; at the same time, they also ask questions energized by the context.

You may notice that there is a rather glaring bit of question-begging or circular reasoning here (to put it in the pejorative senses reserved for it by classical logic): the description assumes the operation of feedback loops whose emergence it was meant to explain — or to put it another way, Hayles participates in the development she describes. My function here — and, I hope, yours too, dear reader — is not to straighten out this circularity but to participate in turn, to weave more loops into the fabric. Enrich the mix beyond the simple dichotomy of science and culture — add capitalism, neurology, literary theory— in any case, a bunch of things that are self-reinforcing — and perhaps ultimately self-limiting or even self-annihilating — into a complex loop, toss lightly and *there you have it*. A metabolism. A culture, describable as a more-or-less *sustainable* self-fulfilling prophecy. An ecology. A chaology.

II. Finding Your Theme Music
Five notes, a bass line, repeated over and over, like a mantra,

from the old Van Morrison song "Into the Mystic," seem to run like an underground stream in my brain, never too far from the surface. Sometimes amid the irregular mental terrain of my perceptions and thoughts and feelings, minute by minute, the stream emerges and flows in the open air for a while before disappearing again, back into some crevasse. Those five notes, set on repeat, feel like a continually secreted hormone that orchestrates some obscure bodily processes. Sometimes it feels so solid, it seems like it should show up on an EEG. Nurse: Doctor, what's this pattern here? Neurologist: Hmm, looks like that old Van Morrison song.

Do you have theme music? I once asked a colleague of mine this question, and she admitted to me that her theme music was the Wicked Witch theme from the *Wizard of Oz*! After that, whenever I saw her walking around campus, I could hear the music — it seemed to orchestrate all of her movements, her attitude, everything.

Be careful about telling people your theme music!

When I was younger, one or more music tracks were always playing in my head, closer to the surface, amid all the other tracks of thoughts and meta-thoughts, perceptions, bodily operational decisions, and so on. I wonder if the multiple music tracks have faded as I've lost some of the excess nervous energy of youth, or is it because multiple generations of personal portable music players have externalized what used to be a brain function? Like many people, I now like walking around the city with my music via earphones. This is a way of wresting back some control over a world that is often chaotic and assaultive; it is a way of choreographing the chaos on behalf of an individualist self ("behold the Great and Powerful Oz!"). Mozart piano concerti are sometimes my feel-good drug, also good at being heard above subway noise. Hard-driving music seems to pump energy continuously to my leg muscles during aerobic exercise, but it has to be soulful. Music provides the soundtrack of who I am, keeps me smiling, moves my legs, makes me think New York City's dancing to *my* beat.

Of course the Muzak company has been taking advantage of this since it was founded in 1935. In addition to its longstanding practice of crafting soundtracks designed to shape people's moods and make them better workers and consumers, the company now sells "audio branding," which involves using what they call the "topology" of a song – "the cultural and temporal associations that it carries with it" – to produce soundtracks for particular stores, that make customers from the target demographic sectors feel that they "belong" there. As senior vice-president Alvin Collis so sensitively puts it, "with audio branding, you're selling emotion, love, caring, feelings."

Scientists who study such things have found that music activates "similar neural systems of reward and emotion as those stimulated by food, sex and addictive drugs," according to a *New York Times* article surveying current scientific approaches to music. Apparently, "the ability to enjoy music has long puzzled biologists because it does nothing evident to help survival": Darwin said that music "must be ranked among the most mysterious" of humankind's abilities. Evolutionary psychologist Steven Pinker (one of the world's leading experts in making sweepingly reductive generalizations, a *very* competitive field) calls music "auditory cheesecake." According to Pinker, music "just happens to tickle several important parts of the brain in a highly pleasurable way, as cheesecake tickles the palate. These include the language ability (with which music overlaps in several ways); the auditory cortex; the system that responds to the emotional signals in a human voice crying or cooing; and the motor control system that injects rhythm into the muscles when walking or dancing." And here's the conclusion: "But since each of these systems evolved for independent reasons, music itself is no more an evolutionary adaptation than is the ability to like dessert, which arises from intense stimulation of the taste buds responsive to sweet and fatty substances." Basically, according to this view, music is just a meme, a fluke, a parasite, a lucky thief who guessed the combination to the safe and has been sneaking off with bits of our precious time and attention ever since.

Imagine where humanity could be now — what diseases we might have cured, what an earthly paradise we might have created — if our attention had not been hijacked by that pernicious parasite, that malicious and satanic meme, music! Presumably this is closely related to why Plato would have banished poets from his ideal republic. Needless to say, though, in such heavens we wouldn't be sitting around playing harps.

The *Times* article also mentions two competing theories, both of which suggest more specific ways that musical ability may have been fostered by natural selection. Maybe music evolved as a form of courtship display, a way that young males signal their fitness to females (soundtrack: "do you love me, now that I can dance?"). Or maybe music has been primarily a way of enacting and enhancing social cohesion, singing and dancing together constituting an extended form of social grooming, a way of asserting group identity against outsiders (soundtrack: *West Side Story*). This is very similar to the story that evolutionary psychology tells about religion.

Whatever their merits, there's a gigantic omission from all of these theories.

One clue can be found in an article that happens to appear on the following page of the *Times*: astronomers have discovered a supermassive black hole in the Perseus galaxy (about 250 million light years from Earth) that is emitting pressure waves 30,000 light years across whose oscillation period is ten million years. The lead astronomer calls this "cosmic hum in B flat" (a B flat 57 octaves lower than middle C) the "lowest note in the universe."

So here's the thing: it's music all the way down, down from culture to our neurological and metabolic rhythms, down to oscillating black holes and subatomic particles made of vibrating strings. Whatever other factors have led to the development of our musical abilities, this has got to be some kind of bottom line. We are musical because we are creatures of a musical universe, in the same way that we are made of matter and energy. That's just what kind of a universe it is. Even the dictionary recognizes the ubiquity of music, defined as "a tone or tones having any or all of the features of rhythm, melody or consonance; melody or harmony generally, as heard in nature or in art."

Accordingly, as you'd expect, humans are not alone in our musicality. Courting pairs of yellow fever mosquitoes are able to harmonize the whine of their wings, at about 1200 hertz, a harmonic of the usual frequency of the male (about 600) and the female (about 400). And, according to one study, even lowly carp can tell the difference between baroque music and the blues, "depressing a button with their snouts to indicate which is which." Now *that* is why I want to be a biologist!

Well, not to seem crass, but so what? If music is so funda-mental, or if the definition of music is so broad, does it really explain anything? Do any particular consequences follow from it? Does it favor certain kinds of theories over others?

Of course, the idea of a musical universe is an ancient one. The notion of "the music of the spheres" relates music to mathe-matics as "universal languages"; that is, logics that lie deeper than the cross-cultural Babel of words and categories, so deep as to constitute the grammar of things themselves, the weaver and the weave of the myriad shapes and forms of the world.

Music, in other words, has worked as a kind of master-concept. A more recent aspirant to the status of master-concept is *information*; that is, the notion that everything in the universe — even matter itself, and certainly music — can be conceptualized as information in its various permutations and transactions — sometimes (as in the work of physicist Stephen Wolfram, mentioned earlier) figured as *computations*. It would be hard to find a starker illustration of Marx's contention that ideas take their shape from the kind of economic system in which they emerge. Is it any wonder that scientists living in what is increasingly known as an "information economy" should start seeing the universe as the same kind of economy, writ large? This is called *economic determinism*.

But my contention about music is precisely the reverse: not that the world seems musical to us because we happen to be addicted to music and our addiction colors how we see the world. Instead, I made the argument that we are musical because the world is musical.

So which is it? And by the same token, should we also say that our trade in information and the predominance of computational processes merely reflect an informational and computational universe? Or is it the other way around?

Believe it or not, I actually have an answer! Are you ready?

Well, for starters, it can't be that human practices simply reflect the musical, informational, or computational universe in which they participate. If that were the case, how come the relative importance of each of these practices — as technologies and as ways of thinking — have varied so dramatically throughout human history? You could try to explain this away by lamenting that it has always been a musical universe, but the hyperspecialization of modern science has made scientists deaf to the music of the spheres, which now only lovers and poets and madmen can hear. Or, on the other hand, you could smugly assert that it has always been an informational and computational universe, but our own science and technology and economics had to reach a certain enlightened state before we could become fully conscious of this fact. Note that these explanations depend on very specific narratives of modernity either as progress, enlightenment, and consciousness-raising — or as decline, alienation, fragmentation, and loss. Both of these kinds of narratives are heavily *teleological* (organized by the notion that history has a *direction*) and even *eschatological* (shaped by a belief in some ultimate destiny of humankind); in other words, they are highly scripted and schematic accounts.

What happens when you try to set aside these reductive teleological and eschatological scripts?

We could start by allowing that different aspects of the universe come to seem dominant to us depending on which of them are economically, conceptually, technologically most important to us at any given point and time. The "us" needs to be used with big scare quotes, since there isn't just one dominant paradigm or one "us" at any given time.

But it also can't be that we simply impose these paradigms on the universe: the question would have to be, from where? Where did these practices and ideas come from? Some Platonic or otherworldly realm? We must have gotten them somehow from the world, selectively, from our worldly interactions and practices, and applied them back again to the world, again selectively. This selectivity makes us who we are, or if you want to take it out of the realm of identity (which makes it seem like a more-or-less fixed thing), this selective looping process continuously makes and remakes both us and our worlds in the process.

Might we find our way from a computational universe to some kind of a musical universe again? One can imagine that such a reconfiguration would get a boost if physicists deploying String Theory discovered that orchestrating sequences of vibrations could alter the fundamental properties of matter, or if neurologists get around to fine-tuning the mood-altering properties of music (which would lead, no doubt, to music copyrights being bought by big pharmaceutical companies), or if we discovered that we could communicate with visiting extraterrestrials using sequences of musical tones (note to self: idea for movie).

So can we find in music a genuine experience of oneness and connection with the universe? It certainly feels that way when you're in the groove. As we've seen, Freud attributed the "oceanic feeling" at the mystical heart of religious experience to the "holding environment" prior to the formation of the individual ego. Or as the British group Cornershop put it, "Everybody needs a bosom for a pillow; everybody needs a bosom; mine's on the 45."

From a psychological perspective, music and mysticism are metaphors for motherhood, but when you take the long view, music came long before mom.

III. Poetics and Autopoietics

i. Preamble

Taking up Professor Lee's injunction to braid the sublime back into the everyday (or to juggle anvils and ping-pong balls together), I now turn to something monstrously grandiose — namely German philosopher Martin Heidegger's influential work *Poetry, Language, and Thought* — as a way to approaching something conspicuously pedestrian: the classic American country song "C-H-I-C-K-E-N," where the Heideggerian poet appears in the guise of backwoods virtuoso Ragtime Joe.

If it works, the world will get turned inside-out and the dazzling grandiosity of the sublime will get redistributed and come to glow through all things. Failing that, I'll be developing (in my usual sideways manner) the question of the continuity of our own complex systems (which here go by the name of *poetics*) with natural self-making systems (*autopoietics*).

Heidegger's work was influential in establishing the priority of language for philosophy — and of understanding language as fundamentally poetic — at a time when poetic, self-referential and performative language tended to be marginalized or stigmatized, even by many of those who study language. Accordingly, Heidegger's work helped spur what is often called the "linguistic turn" in philosophy and cultural theory. All these developments are part of thoroughgoing and ongoing changes in the discursive landscape. In particular, during the late 20th century (as mentioned earlier), poetics and self-reference began becoming important to science again after being banished during its consolidation in the 18th and 19th centuries.

There is a little, um, problem with Heidegger: he was a Nazi. As I see it, even the extent to which his philosophical work is *separable* from his Nazism is a big strike against it: why should we entertain any philosophy or aesthetics that could comfortably coexist with white supremacism and genocide? (Or, not to make it too abstract, why should I read anyone who would have put my mother in a death camp?) But in any case, Heidegger's philosophy and politics were *not* separable: there are profound resonances with Nazi ideology at the core of Heidegger's thought. I have long felt that this renders his work toxic and unusable, but I also understand how this can also make the stakes very high to engage the work, to understand what is compelling about it and to see what can be disentangled from the Nazi-inflected Romanticism also rooted there. Arguably, this is exactly the work begun by the philosophical movement know as deconstruction, and the work that continues — after the linguistic turn — to focus on poetics but without the categorical privileging of language.

Long story short, Planet Heidegger seems to me very bad if you fall into its poisonous atmosphere, but still very good "to think with" — good for the kind of slingshot effect you can get from a close fly-by on your way somewhere else, which is where we're heading here.

ii. Heidegger

In "The Thinker as Poet," Heidegger develops two sets of distinctions, the first among *things*, *equipment*, and *works*, and the second between *earth* and *world*. At least at first, these seem to be elaborations of relatively common-sensical definitions. The thingness of things consists in their being a more or less inert substrate or foundation; they *rest* and *bear*. Equipment consists of things made into tools, characterized by their instrumentality, their being used to perform some action, means to some end. Work is what makes of mere earth a meaningful world, meaning-making.

But such distinctions do not exist at all *until they are named* — by the heroic trio identified in Heidegger's title as *poetry, language,* and *thought.* More than this, "language, by naming beings for the first time, first brings beings to word and to appearance. Only this naming nominates beings *to* their being and *from out of* their being," and by this "projective saying" (exemplified by poetry) creates what Heidegger calls a *world* where there had been only an *earth.* It's easy to protest that poets don't actually create the world, but maybe the best way of getting at Heidegger's point is to say that thought and language *come fully into their own* — that they come to do the work that is most resonantly theirs — only in the work of art or poetry, just as the universe only realizes its potential as it flowers into life and then thought and language.

In one sense, then, distinctions made by thought and language are latecomers in an already-made universe. But thought and language also make for a fundamentally different universe than one in which they are absent, emerging from the material universe and muscling themselves back into it, marshaling and ordering things, breaking them apart and reassembling them. On one hand, the things existed before — for example, there were sounds in the universe before human languages organized sound into phonemes, letters and words — but language takes arbitrary differences and deploys them meaningfully, makes information from noise.

I use this terminology — information from noise — to show how the difference made by language (what I called above a *flowering*) can be understood not only as a subjective or impressionistic claim but also a demonstrable scientific fact. Likewise, when we speak of the *emergence* of language as something new that transforms the context from which it emerges, we recognize again that the ordering principles of language cannot be entirely reduced to or derived from those of the physics and chemistry that preceded them.

Heidegger's distinction between equipment and work focuses on how they handle their materials. The better equipment is, the more it entirely subsumes the "thingness" of the material of which it is made: "the material is all the better and more suitable the less it resists perishing in the equipmental being of the equipment," and "the more handy a piece of equipment is, the more inconspicuous it remains." In contrast, the work of art *highlights* the differences among itself, pure materiality and pure instrumentality. A work of art (such as the Greek temple Heidegger uses as an example),

> in setting up a world, does not cause the material to disappear, but rather causes it to come forth for the very first time and to come into the Open of the work's world. The rock comes to bear and rest and so first becomes rock; metals come to glitter and shimmer, colors to glow, tones to sing, the word to speak. All this comes forth as the work sets itself back into the massiveness and heaviness of stone, into the the firmness and pliancy of wood, into the hardness and luster of metal, into the lighting and darkening of color, into the clang of tone, and into the naming power of the word.

That into which the work sets itself back and which it causes to come forth in this setting back of itself we called the earth.

The work of art — that is, the work that art *does* — to use some of Heidegger's various images, is one of *disclosure*; it creates a *rift* in reality, a *clearing*, in which "some particular entity . . . comes in the work to stand in the light of its being. The being of the being comes into the steadiness of its shining." Or as Leonard

Cohen put it, "there is a crack in everything; that's how the light gets in."

The Heideggerian work of art enacts the striving of world — which "as self-opening cannot endure anything closed" — to surmount the earth — which "as sheltering and concealing, tends always to draw the world into itself and keep it there." The striving of world against earth evokes a late nineteenth-century account of how "upwardly mobile (evolving) biological life appeared in stark relief against an irreversibly decaying thermodynamic universe," a narrative made to resonate "with the white ruling class's sense of themselves, beset inside and out by threats of devolution, degenerescence and disorder." A century later, as befits a neoliberal era, complex systems can be understood less as heroically holding their own against disorder and more as necessarily partnered with chaos, for example, just as so-called dissipative systems (like living things) surf on their own dissolution.

Accordingly, if Heideggerian categories can be deployed without the grandiosity ("under erasure," in the deconstructionist phrase), they are still useful in approaching the work of art. Artists *work their materials* — of if you want to put this in the most demystifying way possible, you could say that a painter (for example) is someone who pushes paint around on a canvas.

Once, while walking around a big show of surrealist painting in 2002, I was struck by the wisdom of this otherwise diffident formula when I began focusing on the brush strokes. A Dali painting, I noticed, had mostly been made additively, more like a collage: upon a background a figure is added — laid on top — and then additional features are added to the figure, and so on. On the other hand, Miro had used a conspicuous variety of techniques to work edges and interfaces: the brushstrokes tell you that one figure lays on top of another, like a boat cutting through water, while both the background and figure sides of another edge have been reworked with parallel brushstrokes, as if they were two equivalent kinds of entities rubbing up to each other, while at yet another edge the background seems to be *on top* of the figure, like a wave lapping onto a beach. It seems as if, having discovered this variable, the artist — and art collectively, including the very different tack taken by the Dali paintings — is driven to explore all possible permutations, as flowing water finds all possible routes around a set of obstacles.

It is fitting that one of the common images for such a range of expressive possibilities is taken from painting: the *palette*. The image of water flowing downhill works as another antidote to Heidegger's fascist-inflected account of heroic striving and surmounting.

iii. Ragtime Joe

Heidegger's terms will help us approach the work of the poet as practiced by the character known as Ragtime Joe in the song "C-H-I-C-K-E-N," a traditional song adapted and made popular by American country musician "Uncle Dave" Macon in the 1920s, while Heidegger was working on his own greatest hit, *Being and Time.*

The song opens with the image of a country schoolhouse — that icon of modernity establishing its dominion over nature and tradition — but even here the poet continues to reside. The children are undergoing a spelling lesson, standing in for all the literacies and technical knowledges demanded by modernity. But there is also, in the face of this demand, a collective failure that will reveal the poverty at the heart of modern knowledge, since it is in the wake of this failure that we must call again upon the poet, who jumps in where purely instrumental knowledge fears to tread:

> In a little country school house where the children used to go,
> There lived a little feller by the name of Ragtime Joe.
> One day the teacher called on the class to spell a certain

kind of bird,
The kind of bird is a chicken, and they could not spell that
    word.

The teacher called on Ragtime Joe to spell that word for
    them,
He did not hesitate a bit, this is the way he began:
C - that's the way to begin
H - that's the next letter in
I - that is the third
C - season to the bird
K - filling it in
E - getting near the end
C-H-I-C-K-E-N; that is the way to spell chicken.

The success of art and virtuosity in the wake of the failure of
instrumental rationality is a familiar Romantic narrative, but the
song doesn't stop here. In the second verse, the schoolhouse is
given back over to music and poetry, but art generally and the
artist himself are also shown to fail when instrumentalized in
turn as hired entertainment. As Walter Benjamin put it, "in every
era the attempt must be made anew to wrest tradition away from
a conformism that is about to overpower it." The poet must then
return to his genuine calling:

Parson Johnson gave a concert in the old school house one
    night,
He hired lots of talent that could sing and could recite;
When they pulled the curtain, everything went wrong
Until the children loudly called, "Let's hear from Ragtime
    Joe."

He sang a ragtime jukin' tune, but it did not go so well,
He said, "I went 'cross on that, so I guess I'll have to spell,"

He told the audience he had composed this chicken song
And when he sang these words to them, he took the house
by storm:

[Chorus]

There is something about the spelling song that seems to tickle actual listeners, and we can imagine that this is how Ragtime Joe was able first to win the day in class and then to take the house by storm. Part of this charm must derive from Joe getting away with singing during spelling class, sneaking play back into work (as recognized in the slogan "art is whatever you can get away with"). We can also be charmed by the way the poet makes art out of the most pedestrian and unpromising materials (as in the Book of Matthew: "The stone that the builders rejected has become the cornerstone . . . and it is wonderful in our eyes").

But the magic trick that charms us when we hear the song is less music breaking out in the middle of spelling than spelling breaking out in the middle of music. The song enacts language taking itself apart, showing us the materials of which it is made while not ceasing to function as language: it opens itself up to reveal its beating heart. The poet shows us the letters of the word, sequenced to the simple ascending notes of a musical scale, both woven into the words and music of which they are the elements. As Heidegger puts it, the poet shows us how "earth juts through the world and world grounds itself on earth."

So the heart of the song is its disclosure of its own materials, the letters of language and the scale of music. It situates itself at the hinge where *thing* is opened up into *work*, putting us in touch with its material substrate.

Equally important, it is also a *meta-song*; a song about a song. Imagine a performer on stage singing the song, which tells the story of the song's composition, and (in the second verse) features a performer on stage telling his audience the story of his song's composition: it's a *meta-meta-song*. And by the way, Uncle Dave Macon first performed professionally, in 1921, as part of a church benefit show in a Tennessee schoolhouse.

On the one hand, we could say that the way the song conspicuously spans and loops together several levels, sub to meta (showing us *things* — being converted into *means* — to manufacture *meaning*), distinguishes it as an exemplary Heideggerian artwork. On the other hand, this spanning and looping is how we recognize its kinship with other complex, recursive systems, including language itself, and other living creatures.

Why is it important that Ragtime Joe does not "hesitate a bit" when called on? It certainly speaks to his virtuosity, but the song doesn't tell us whether the idea to sing-and-spell came suddenly upon him, like a bolt out of the blue, or whether he may have long had the idea and was merely waiting for the right opportunity to try it. In any case, the moment has something of the absoluteness of a beginning. As Heidegger puts it, "this unmediated character of a beginning, the peculiarity of a leap out of the unmediable, does not exclude but rather includes the fact that the beginning prepares itself for the longest time and wholly inconspicuously," or as Hamlet said, "readiness is all."

The humblest instance may capture it best: when you are a student called on to speak in class, you can't be absolutely sure what will come out of your mouth, or how — you just have to start talking. Rather than "finding your voice" or "expressing yourself," the challenge is to "*lose* yourself in the music, the moment" as Eminem put it. I suspect that Eminem may have been thinking of literary theorist Roland Barthes' description of the act of writing as "the destruction of every voice, of every point of origin. Writing is that neutral, composite, oblique space where our subject slips away, the negative where all identity is lost." What is required is less inspiration and something more like courage or even *abandon*: one must simply throw oneself into the situation, like a flash flood making its headlong path.

There is another kind of leap at the end of spelling the word. Notice that no separate account is given for the final letter — the "n" at the end of *chicken* — as is provided for each of the preceding letters. It is as if the pieces cease to be fully accountable as pieces as they come to constitute the whole, as the letters become the word. After our descent to earth, we seamlessly rejoin the world. This speaks to the relationship between means and meaning, or between becoming and being, that is also the subject of an old Yiddish joke:

> A child has a pathological fear of kreplach, the dumpling that is a staple of East-European Jewish cooking. A psychologist recommends to the mother that she carefully explain the making of kreplach to the child, so that he will be able to see that his fears are groundless. She sits him down at the table and shows him each successive step: now I'm rolling out the dough, now I'm cutting it, now I'm putting in the filling, now I'm folding over the first edge, and so on. Prompted at the completion of each step, the child calmly indicates, "okay, mama," but as she says "now I'm folding over the final edge," the child leaps up screaming in horror, "Ach! Kreplach!"

No matter how carefully prepared in advance, the world of meaning is ultimately born or re-entered through "a leap out of the unmediable."

One fundamental question remains: why chicken? — not in kreplach, I mean, but in the song. Why not any other kind of bird, or any other kind of word?

In addressing this question, I want to avoid the kind of "Just So Story" that Edgar Allan Poe tells in his famous essay, "The Art of Composition." Poe seems to demonstrate that any poet — merely by using a set of objective principles to make the best

selections among an infinity of topics, techniques and forms —
will inevitably come to compose the poem "The Raven." This
rather silly bit of narcissism (deployed with some irony by Poe,
one suspects) serves at least to remind us that, especially in
Romantic and post-Romantic poetry, birds and birdsong are
commonly used reflexively to represent poets and poetry. Of
course a chicken doesn't sing but only clucks and squawks,
making it all the more fitting a figure for the song's proud
humility, edging into self-mockery — a stance characteristic of
much American folk music. There are also obvious resonances
between chicken pecking and clucking and guitar and banjo
picking and plucking. Various versions of the song make a point
of exaggerating these resonances. In any case, this reflexivity — a
signature feature especially of Romantic and post-Romantic
poetry — must be part of the multiple factors that determine the
choice of the word *chicken*.

Of course there are plenty of other spelling songs that do *not*
feature the word *chicken*. I'm thinking of the sentimental 1915
song "M-O-T-H-E-R," country-western singer Tammy Wynette's
"D-I-V-O-R-C-E," and Van Morrison's classic rock song "G-L-O-
R-I-A." The fact that each of these, like the chicken song, uses
words of six or seven letters and two or three syllables seems to
indicate that something about the standard rhythms, meters, and
line lengths of American song makes these words work especially
well. It is a rather obvious and uncontroversial observation: the
words are sonically and otherwise well adapted to their poetic
environments, in fact are *naturally selected* for this reason. What is
remarkable here is that this is a serviceable definition of poetry
no less than of biological evolution. This is not to say that there
cannot be spelling songs based on shorter or longer words —
quite the opposite: it suggests that all viable adaptational niches
will tend to be explored, in poetry no less than in biology.

But there is another much more specific reason why an iconic
spelling lesson might well include the word *chicken*. The funda-

mental deployment of language, in the Judeo-Christian tradition, is Adam's naming the creatures.

So here's the punchline. It seems that the first linguistic act of humankind, according to the *Book of Genesis* anyway, may well have included a word for chicken:

> Out of the ground the Lord God formed every beast of the field, and every fowl of the air, and brought them unto the man to see what he would call them, and whatsoever the man called every living creature, that was the name thereof.

God's word — *logos* — constitutes his agency in creating the world; creation is represented as a performative, projective speech act (e.g., "let there be light"). Man is created in God's image, and language, by "naming beings for the first time" (as Heidegger put it) enacts man's world-creating power. *Genesis* is very specific about the absolute performative sovereignty of language as naming: "whatsoever the man called every living creature, that was the name thereof"; the implication is that even God has to wait and see what names Adam would invent. This absoluteness characterizes what deconstruction calls *phallogocentrism*, by which patriarchal power is linked to the deification of language and the domination of humans over other creatures.

Because of the understanding of language as naming, people are much more likely to associate the first steps in teaching language (whether speaking or spelling) with nouns rather than verbs. The tendency to think of the most elemental words as nouns —including what might occur to us as a child's first words — such as *mama*, *papa*, *doggie*, etc. — is part of a general conceptual framework that situates material things as noun-like building blocks.

The poverty of this view is stunning. It is inconceivable (for example) that the word *mama*, when first uttered by a child,

could ever be a simple noun rather than some kind of action —
an act of separation, a recognition, a demand for union —
something with some push and pull — in what is already a
complex network of directions and trajectories of desires — well
before these come to be personified in self and other, before
coalescing into a grammar divided into nouns and verbs, subjects
and objects and so on.

But the performativity of language is precisely Heidegger's
point: that language distinguishes itself as dynamic by thingi-
fying things, making the earth an earth and the ground a ground
by situating itself over and above them — smart words and dumb
things — by pushing everything else down, claiming verbal
agency by making everything else into a noun. This dialectic, the
production of this hierarchized binary opposition, is wired into
the core logic of capitalism and colonialism: imperial power and
colony, mental and physical work, management and labor,
bourgeoisie and proletariat, and later, information and industrial
economy. Here in particular we can appreciate that it will not
work to avoid Heidegger, since our language and thought are
riddled with these polarities; hence, the ongoing necessity of
deconstruction.

Notice that there is a paradox in the view that language is
performative; that it works primarily to *do* something and only
secondarily to *refer* to something. The paradox can be succinctly
stated: the verb comes first, but only by distinguishing that which
is distinguished — the noun — *as first*. The temporal paradox
here can be understood as a feature of the emergence of complex
systems that manufacture their own components, as languages
make the phonic distinctions they use as signifying elements, and
as living creatures manufacture their own cells, chemicals, genes,
etc. This is the underlying meaning of *beginning again*.

Would it be egregious to point out here that we generally refer
to this temporal paradox as *the chicken and egg problem*?

Chapter Five

Ending and Returning

I. Road Trip With(out) Professor Lee

If we go on in this way, then even the cleverest mathematician can't tell where we'll end, much less an ordinary man. If by moving from nonbeing to being we get to three, how far will we get if we move from being to being? (Chuang Tzu)

Writing and reading and driving: the parallels are obvious. The parallels: get it? Reading and writing and driving are, in fact, paralellizing technologies; that is, *channelings*: ways of making straight lines out of the otherwise wandering and wayward activities of thought, communication, and movement through space. There can be something sinister about this—the disciplining of a jazzy dance into a military march, the impoverishment of multiple self-orchestrating dimensions into a single rigid line—but only when this mode comes to dominate. Otherwise there's a balance, an ecology: the linear does not necessarily squeeze out the nonlinear but can enable and enhance it: think of the human body and brain with their multiple channeled, linearized flows and complex, nonlinear choreographies. Did the spread of literacy exalt book-learning to the detriment of other kinds of knowledges, resulting in some general impoverishment of humanity, or did it enable the proliferation of new knowledges and ways of being and experiencing the world? Yes and yes. Do highways homogenize or diversify the world? Yes and yes again.

i. Triborough Bridge

Early one morning in May, I set off from my apartment in Brooklyn on a 1200-mile road trip, alone. This is the trip that I had been planning to make with Professor Lee. Over three days, I'll drive through New York State, up and over the Great Lakes, across southern Ontario, and down through Minnesota to my old home town, Minneapolis.

But as it happens, five minutes after setting off, I'm just inching along in a traffic jam on the Brooklyn-Queens Expressway. Above me — on a bridge that spans the Expressway — a stooped, white-bearded, rabbinical old man haltingly makes his way.

A few miles on, in Queens, the traffic starts speeding along again, but the road is under construction and I'm not sure which lane leads to the Triborough Bridge. This makes me anxious, and I start yelling to myself, in a series of phony accents, "Where's the Triborough Bridge? Where's the goddamn Triborough?" And then the answer: "It's right where it always was, asshole." This calms me down by throwing me into a silent meditation on the multiple meanings of the word *where*.

Crossing the bridge to the Bronx triggers two memories that wash over me in quick succession.

First I remember how, several weeks earlier, I finally found a way out of a period of insomnia that had lasted many weeks when I was stressed out at work. I was exhausted, but somehow I could never quite access the tiredness. One night, lying in bed and unable to sleep, it occurred to me that I was two people, one all jazzed up and the other dead tired. It wasn't my body that was tired and my mind that was awake, since the exhaustion had both mental and physical aspects, and so did the wakefulness. Then the phrase *I am the bridge* occurred to me as a kind of mantra, and it was like opening up a lock or a valve: I felt equilibrium being restored, like water seeking its own level, and relaxation flooding through me.

Then I am surprised by the memory of another bridge: the Mississippi River bridge from which, about ten years earlier, I had scattered my mother's ashes. It was early September. I had just finished a book manuscript and was about to send it to my publisher, also based in Minneapolis, when I got the call about my mother. I flew from New York, borrowed an old friend's van, drove to the funeral home, and sat for a while with my mother's body. The next day I delivered the book manuscript to my editor, stopping on the way to pick up my mother's ashes, then drove through my old home town, the back of the rattling old van empty except for the manuscript and the box of ashes. I dropped off the manuscript on the way to my mother's memorial service. That evening I drove to the Lake Street Bridge, parked nearby and walked to the middle of the bridge, where I stood in one of the little niches that projected out over the water. I remembered to check the wind direction, as a friend had cautioned me, before scattering the ashes. Night had just fallen. I had no prayer, not even a goodbye. So I just stood for what seemed like a respectful interval, then opened the lid and shook the ashes out over the water far below. Lit by a streetlight, the ashes began to descend, a luminous white cloud, and then, caught by some mysterious updraft, the still luminous cloud ascended, dispersing, and was gone.

These two memories, which strike me now as moments of almost miraculously being brought back to the here-and-now from far away, bring me back again to myself. It is a sunny morning in May. I am driving across the Triborough Bridge.

ii. Ontario

Late in the evening, I stop at a motel west of Toronto and try to call Iona but discover that my cellphone doesn't work in Canada. I had anticipated this possibility and warned her that I might not be able to call. Even so, during the whole drive through Ontario, I'll be dogged by a low-level anxiety: off the grid!

Just after dawn the next morning, I set off from the motel. A few miles on, I notice three radio towers in a field. Two of them line up for a moment as I pass. It occurs to me that any two points can be lined up with some third point, but no perspective can be found to line up *three* points unless they're in a line already. My mind begins to squirm to find a way around this rather obvious principle. It occurs to me that they could line up if space itself were curved, as in the neighborhood of a black hole.

Much later, I will think that it must have been here, inspired in some subtle way by the radio towers, that I began to compose the poem I will keep whittling in my mind, off and on, for the whole journey. I will come to call the poem "Road Trip." Eventually it settles down to three lines of five words each, something like the old Burma Shave billboards:

Children want to stop everywhere.
Adults want to keep driving.
The old make wry observations.

It amuses me to characterize myself as old. It seems like a quaint affectation, even though *I really am old*. It will occur to me only long after I have returned home that the poem echoes the otherwise somewhat random observation about the radio towers. The first two lines of the poem are opposite and aligned, and the third is askew, curving back on the first two.

I'm like a field in which there are three radio towers.

Many miles beyond the towers, the highway is under construction. New lanes are being built parallel to the existing road. Immense trucks and tractors move like insects over the landscape. My journey has been so long, everything looks small to me.

Driving along Highway 17, I pass the town of Spanish and can't get it out of my head. What's so endearing about a name that's an adjective? I think of Professor Lee, whose surname is a suffix that makes all adjectives into adverbs, and it makes me laugh. It's the first time I've thought of *professorly* as a word. It makes me laugh — a little posthumous gift from him.

After a while, I pass a big green A-frame building labeled TRADING POST and promising NATIVE CRAFTS, and a few miles farther along, a colorful billboard for BARB'S EMBROIDERY, and a few miles farther, at the entrance to a ramshackle group of trailers, a sign for LAIRD'S SIGNS. The word *SIGNS* is lettered in huge block capitals on its own billboard, and beneath it hangs a large banner printed with the word *BANNERS*. The signs and trailers are in such disrepair that it makes me wonder if the whole enterprise may have been abandoned years before.

I start imagining that I'm passing through some kind of legendary Village of Fools where everybody tries to eke out a living by bartering signs to each other. After a while I start daydreaming that Professor Lee is sitting next to me and turns to me and says, if I'm not mistaken, Watson, keep your eye out for an old man wearing a cap embroidered with the name LAIRD.

A few miles along, a sign offering MONUMENTS presides over a yard full of gravestones. Holmes, I say, cocking my head: perhaps you'll find your man over yonder.

Many miles further along, I pass a motel with a sign out front that reads

MOTEL
BREAKFAST
WELCOME TRAVELERS!

The desolate motel makes the welcome seem positively poignant. It may not be much, I think, but at least here's someone peddling something a little more solid than words. I imagine Barb and Laird sitting together silently over breakfast. Then I imagine an exchange with a motel clerk. Do you have internet connections? Nope. Can I make a long-distance call? Nope. Got an ice machine? Look mister, like the sign says, we've got a motel and we've got breakfast.

At this moment, the world seems both heartbreakingly hard and exhilaratingly easy. What a hard world where this desolate outpost passes for an oasis! And what an easy world where you can make a living with just a sign, some bedrooms, and some little boxes of cereal!

Barreling along at top speed through the Teutonic forests of western Ontario, I remember the traffic jam on the Brooklyn-Queens Expressway with the rabbinical old man hobbling slowly across the bridge overhead.

Miles on, the imaginary hotel clerk is still speaking to me. Look, mister, you come through here at a hundred kilometers an hour and you think you know anything at all about us?

I imagine a town called Laconic, Ontario.

iii. Minnesota

The next day is misty all along the North Shore of Lake Superior. Forests of birch in new leaf emerge from the mist, and from among them, dark and towering old Norway pines.

I wonder how I know they are Norway pines, and also, in spite of the name, that they don't grow in Norway. It occurs to me that the trees must have been named by Norwegian immigrants who recognized in them a fantasy of the Old Country.

I remember how, when growing up, I always used to think of northern Minnesota as a wilderness beyond the reaches of civilization. I remember walking — I couldn't have been more than eight at the time — with my father and Professor Lee in an old-growth pine forest on Madeleine Island, in Lake Superior, and my father quoting Longfellow: "this is the forest primeval." Remarkable that this would be one of just a handful of memories I have of my father: a little agate, plucked from the rushing stream. The elder Professor Livingston is long gone, and now

Professor Lee. Nobody reads Longfellow anymore. Not even me. In fact, I wonder how I even know that it was Longfellow my father was quoting.

In a few months, I will be older than my father ever was.

The northern forests still have some of the romance of my childhood. Their strangeness is familiar to me, but now, coming home, I feel that I have always been a stranger here.

I think of the end of the film *Alien Resurrection*. Ripley, a cloned human-alien hybrid, and a cyborg robot named Analee, have spent their entire lives off-world. As their spaceship descends into sunlit clouds and the music swells, they see Earth for the first time. It's beautiful, Analee says, then asks Ripley what to expect. I don't know, Ripley says, downbeat. I'm a stranger here myself.

I cross the border and re-enter the United States. More forests of pine and birch.

Speeding up a long hill, it suddenly seems to me that I can see every leaf and needle on every tree, like a nearsighted teenager with his first pair of glasses. Ahead, the road goes up and up and disappears into the mist.

And then I find myself crying without quite knowing why, wiping away the tears, crying and driving, and then laughing and crying, and driving. And then, in the little melodrama of the moment, something else seems to be amping up the hysteria, something deeply disconcerting, like some weird hallucination of a presence with me in the car. I immediately think of Professor Lee, but then I realize that it is an actual physical sensation, a sound: next to me, in the passenger's seat, my cellphone is ringing.

II. Waking Up In Beijing

i.

A dream: we are dismantling an office, taking apart big old metal furniture, removing decades worth of files and accumulated junk. I wander off in search of more cardboard boxes. Eventually I enter a grand but shabby house on top of a hill and begin talking with the owner. We have an ironic conversation in which we both know we're not really having the conversation we're pretending to have. At the same time, though, I don't know exactly what we *are* talking about. I think: this must be what is meant by *unconscious communication*.

Then I go out, walking down the hill, alongside some concrete steps that have become a stream-bed. Walking gives way to flying, and I am gliding along now, smoothly, inches above the ground, which is covered, like a baroque upholstered fabric, in what seem to be *green peppers*.

ii.

Light traffic noise, muffled bustling, and through the light fabric hung over the window, the light itself, the first light of morning, suffuses the room, giving me the sense of both immersion and removal, as if the noise and light, eddying softly around me, were cocooning me, just on the nightside of dawn and the dreamside of waking.

iii.

I remember Professor Lee speculating about what would it be to write a book in which you gave all the good lines to *others*. Not by caricaturing the narrator as an imbecile, he told me, but much more subtly, just so that, at every point where the reader might find himself nodding slowly in silent assent, in the receipt of some sublime insight, it would have been delivered by someone other than the narrator.

I said that this could only seem like a surprising perspective to a scholar used to delivering the wisdom himself, but it could hardly be news to a novelist. The Professor laughed and he agreed but said the real insight lay in how such a third-person voice would embody one of several different ways of understanding what's going on as you read.

In the first of these, I, the reader of these lines — I mean the one who is at this very moment reading this very line — am myself the writer, or should be considered as such. I am not a mere actor reading lines that have been written for me—but then, neither is the actor, who makes the lines truly his own or else is not much of an actor! But furthermore, the book is not exactly the lines written herein, but rather the thoughts in my head as I read, the book I write as I read.

For example, this notion — that another book is being written, simultaneously, by the reader — echoes what the narrator was saying earlier about unconscious communication, something from one of his dreams ("we're not really having the conversation we're pretending to have"). So is it my own thought, or did some other writer plant the seed in me?

Sometimes for many lines, whole passages in fact, my thoughts seem to coincide with what is written in the book, but then I notice that another line of thought has been running alongside, and then another sprouts out at a sharp angle, and another I can't quite make out skulks along like a shadow at some remove.

Hey, you there! Yeah, you! Are you following me? Go ahead, come out, let me see you! Come on, I know you're there!

And it wasn't some writer, other than myself I mean, whose magic wand stirred up these ripples in me, who peopled my mind with these jugglers and clowns. They are mine, and this is, must be, *my book*, because *all that I am capable of thinking are my own thoughts*. And because all that I am capable of thinking are my own thoughts, *these* are my own thoughts too. And when I say *I* and *me*, of course I still mean *I who am reading these lines*.

Or then again, should we say instead that a very wise man, *not me*, wrote these lines? Or at least, so I like to think. Here in these lines I encounter another, and my reading is my engagement with this other. Perhaps the writer is not wise but merely *another*. Perhaps wisdom is merely in engaging another, and the writer is one of those who knows how to do this.

iv.

Back to another dream: I'm on a bus now, speeding through a city, and multiple lanes of traffic, as far as the eye can see in either direction, are speeding alongside me. But up in front, maybe a hundred yards ahead, I see perpendicular traffic speeding along, as if we were fast approaching a red light at an intersection with an equally immense mega-superhighway at rush hour. I brace for catastrophic impact. But instead of screeching to a stop and instead of crashing we continue moving through the perpendicular traffic, all the vehicles somehow — improbably — missing each other.

It occurs to me later that this is a dream version of Beijing traffic, with its cyclists and pedestrians crossing through lanes of cars at giant intersections.

v.

Here in Beijing fashion at the moment, Xiao Yu told me, anything goes. I have noticed teenage girls wearing t-shirts that have contrasting half-vests sewn on; to my eye it looks like fashion-victim stuff from the 1980s. Women seem to wear high heels with everything. And carry umbrellas in the hot sun. I see skirts over pants, contrasting patterns, fake tatters, tortoiseshell frames with no lenses, hot pants, couples with matching t-shirts. Then again, lots of men are wearing chinos and polo shirts, over and over, just like in the US. But some of them are also carrying what look to me like purses.

A workman, shirtless and with a rose tattooed on his upper arm, is smoking and cursing with his buddies on their break. Old men in old-school Chinese army jackets.

Contrary to the classic Western caricature of the Chinese as massively conformist, their anarchism is also a leading characteristic. Or so says Professor Lee.

vi.

My thoughts, all of these thoughts, it occurs to me, are like the froth and spray of waves, the dark water welling up among the craggy black rocks. The surfaces of the massive swells are scalloped, like pounded metal — tiled like a drying mud puddle into curling, tilting, pointy-cornered pieces — and where they slap up against the rocks, meringue-like bits of foam and explosions of spray, propelled irresistibly by the whole sea pushing behind them, splash up and then wash back down along the rocks, trickling back down through the clinging seaweed and barnacles and all the niches bubbling with life: "The poem of the mind in the act of finding what will suffice."

vii.

And then this gloss: the narrator's thoughts, while waking up, seem to go every which way, every way they can, like the tilting surfaces of the waves. He downplays their significance, making them out to be nothing more than ephemeral froth or spray — a very Chinese gesture, one might say. And yet they take place, with considerable drama — splashily, one might say — in some kind of interzone, between sleep and waking, a beach, a place of flux, where rock is being eroded into sand and evolving life simmers in crevasses and tide pools.

There is something poignant about the image: the sea, destined forever to strain at its edge, pulled as if by a longing that traverses its entire being ("the whole sea pushing"), flings itself against its limits, again and again and again, like a wild animal pacing in its cage. And yet, something comes of this sustained exercise in futility; it is somehow fundamentally creative, like the tides of Chinese fashion mentioned earlier, conformity and anarchism somehow occurring together, the little tilting surfaces of the greater tilting and swelling surface, each pulled irresistibly along, each with their degrees of freedom.

"The poem of the mind in the act of finding what will suffice." What the narrator seems to be saying, by ending with the famous first lines of the 1940 Wallace Stevens poem, "Of Modern Poetry," is that this book — that is, the one you are reading now — is also describable as "the poem of the mind in the act of finding what will suffice." The sentence has no verb; it functions as a complex noun, but this—along with the phrase "in the act of finding" — makes us realize that the whole phrase is a kind of gerund or participle, a verb that functions as a noun. A poem is just such a thing that is not a thing but a process.

But why "of the mind?" Is this a purely cognitive exercise? Maybe Stevens did over-emphasize the cognitive. But we may also understand something more like *mind and mindfulness as ways of being*, and even beyond this, as creative and reflexive principles that belong to the universe, not to humans alone. And perhaps we should follow the suggestion that whatever the mind would be finding would have to be something other than mind, something like the mystical "palm at the *end* of the mind, *beyond* the last thought," about which Stevens wrote many years later.

"In the act of finding" is a perfect example of what Professor Lee means by a *stance*: not a frozen posture, but the paradox of always being in the act of finding without ever having found, again not a noun but a gerund. To find, not as if it were simply laying there to be found, but something that is both found and, simultaneously, made.

And "what *will* suffice," anyway? Thanks, Mr. Stevens, for so pointedly *not* making the search into some kind of striving for perfection, which anyway now sounds like part of the whole corporate "search for excellence" bullshit, like something from a car commercial. What will suffice is not perfection, but something sustaining and sustainable — perhaps the act of finding, in itself?

At every moment, by putting out feelers, by doomed and dogged and even depressive repetition, like the sea at its edge, and yet always new, always breaking through into —

viii.

Now.

And now, in the now of writing, I suddenly remember standing—in February or March of 1990, it would have been — about twenty years ago, at this writing — outside Newark, Ohio—on a low, dry-grass-covered earthen mound in the shape of a stylized bird with wings outspread. I had come to nearby Dennison University for a job interview, and someone had taken me to see the mounds. The bird had been made, my host told me, by the people known now as Hopewell, something like 2000 years earlier.

After a gauntlet of interviews, in a series of stuffy rooms, with everybody trying to sound smart and attentive, it felt like a revelation to be outside, walking and standing, mostly in silence, among the cold and windswept mounds.

I stood for a while on the back of this bird that, for 2000 years, has been flying through time.

I don't know what it looked like when it was first made. Perhaps it had a crisper outline, and more realistic details— feathers, talons, an eye — or perhaps not. It has been being made and unmade ever since. As it flies through time, it gets more and more streamlined by erosion; by the desultory forces of wind, water, worms, and walkers. It becomes more and more stylized. Its flight is a disappearance. And yet, it seems to me, it was and is and will be *perfect at every moment of its existence*. Now it is low, just a few feet high, sloping gently into the surrounding ground, and one might walk over it unknowing, without noticing, poised as it is so perfectly between culture and nature.

How would you describe its journey? As a kind of one-way

time machine, a voyaging out into the future? Or as a return, a long detour on the way home, ashes to ashes?

Does it seem poignant to you, tragic, or joyful, or calm?

ix.

Back on the all-day train from Shanghai to Beijing, China rolled by like a scroll, a vast and horizontal landscape of fields, villages and cities disappearing into the haze.

Two magpies, startled by the train, fly up and over the poplars that line the track, one slightly ahead of the other. Lotuses crowd at the edge of big muddy ponds, craning their necks as if at odds with their own rootedness. A goatherd walks through a field with his scrawny flock, while a train passes over them on an elevated track, each of its yellow cars marked with a death's head. Under an overpass in a gray city, amid scattered small heaps of picked-through garbage, built against the bridge supports, ramshackle lean-tos made of broken bricks and sticks and scraps so small it makes me wonder where the more privileged dump-dwellers live. At the birthplace of Confucius, a garish golden statue of the sage stands on top of a tourist center at the foot of the holy mountain fading into the fog. The grimy backside of a carnival midway.

Small groups of workers, and some solitary workers — the rest have left for the cities — in wheat fields and rice paddies and on dirt roads and tracks, chopping with a hoe, walking with a big wooden pitchfork, harvesting wheat, stooped over and weeding, riding an old tractor, riding a bicycle, a motorcycle.

Small, scattered groups of workers toil variously in a field, while a magpie watches from an electrical line.

A shepherd rests with her flock in a small grove of trees.

At the edge of a field, just where it begins to slope down to a marshy stream alongside the tracks, at the end of long, bending bamboo poles, someone has set out two red lanterns.

III. Still Knitting

But this has not been and still is not a *story*. It's not any kind of *narrative*.

You could try to make what I've just said into a story by saying, "he said it wasn't a story, then he said I could try to make it into a story, and then I proceeded to do just that."

Though you've parceled out the dialogue and actions to a couple of characters (a writer and a reader), and even though you've framed it as a series of events in a time sequence, it's *still* not a story, since that's not the level where the interesting things are happening, the things that make this what it is — which, as I keep telling you, is *not a story*!

Now here's some dialogue for you, dear reader: you keep saying *you, you, you*, and making out like *I'm* the one who wants to make a story out of everything, but *it ain't me, babe*: nobody's parceled out any dialogue but you, author dearest, and up till now you haven't even given me any lines! But I'll humor you for the moment: if it's not a story, what is it?

Okay, thanks for asking. Let me give you an example. Let's say the sky opens up and you see a vision of a chariot with four creatures, each with four faces — or maybe not a chariot but a kind of gyroscope, and maybe not four creatures but a three-dimensional chalkboard teeming with dancing equations — or maybe not a gyroscope and a chalkboard, but in any case, let's say that you are overwhelmed, in that moment, with the sense of the cosmic meaning of the vision, whatever it might be. Later, you try to tell a friend about it, and you try to tell it as a story: I was walking along, and then the sky opened up, and so on. But you know that the story *about* the vision doesn't even begin to capture either the experience or the meaning of the vision, which is the only thing you really want to *deliver* to your friend, as it was delivered to you. But a story *about* something, anything, is by definition *not* the thing in question. In fact, it often functions as a way of distancing one from the thing in question.

So for now, let's just say that what I'm talking about here *is* part of the thing in question, it is the delivering and the doing of the thing in question or the questioning of the thing in question. I'm *not* telling you a story about some vision I had, and it's not because there is no vision to be had: it's because this *is* the vision, this, right here and now, in my writing and your reading of these sentences — or as you would say, in *your* writing and *my* reading! *This* is what's happening, and while we can negotiate a conventional way of assigning dialogue and agree that "I" will refer to the reader and "you" to the writer (for example) — it doesn't matter, because what's really happening is in the intersubjective realm of meaning between us.

There is an official convention of using the present tense in writing about fiction. In everyday usage, we tend to mix tenses when recounting a fictional story, but the baseline is supposed to be all present. Writing about the film *Frankenstein*, for example, one might say: after the monster is brought down from the roof, he moves his hand, and Frankenstein jumps back and starts saying "it's alive; it's alive," and so on. The reason for using all present, at least as I've been told, is to distinguish the "eternal present" of fiction from the past, present, and future of real time. The original film of Frankenstein was made in 1931 (note the past tense *was*, since the making of the film occurred in real, historical time), but every time anyone watches it, in 1931 or 2031, the monster moves his hand and the doctor says "it's alive" in the present tense — and keeps on saying it, in fact, which is why the film *really is alive*!

William Blake gave the odd name *Golgonooza* to the timeless realm of art. As Northrop Frye described it (in *Fearful Symmetry*),

> All imaginative and creative acts, being eternal, go to build up a permanent structure, which Blake calls Golgonooza, above time, and, when this structure is finished, nature, its scaffolding, will be knocked away and man will live in it.

Golgonooza will then be the city of God, the New Jerusalem which is the total form of all human culture and civilisation. Nothing that the heroes, martyrs, prophets and poets of the past have done for it has been wasted; no anonymous and unrecognised contribution to it has been overlooked. In it is conserved all the good man has done, and in it is completed all that he hoped and intended to do.

As you've gathered, I'm not much of a time guy either — which is why my field is poetics, not narrative. As Allen Ginsberg said, I'm one of those people "who threw their watches off the roof to cast their ballot for Eternity outside of Time, and alarm clocks fell on their heads every day for the next decade."

To put this into theoretical perspective, you have to back up a bit.

The movement known as Structuralism in cultural theory began in linguistics and anthropology about a hundred years ago but had a very wide-ranging influence over many fields. Structuralism was famously good at looking at static snapshots of the architecture of systems, such as language or culture, much less good at thinking about time and change and growth.

When structuralists think about system change beyond what can be accommodated by simple gradualism — in which the snapshots are arranged into a kind of flip-book — they often see crisis, rupture and revolution. This is why anthropologist Mary Douglas ends her classic structuralist book *Purity and Danger* with a chapter called "The System Shattered and Renewed." This is why Thomas Kuhn wrote about long periods of what he called "normal science" punctuated by revolutionary paradigm shifts. And this is why Foucault, even as he became a poststructuralist, remained committed to the notion of systemic "ruptures" in ways of thinking and knowing.

When you're focused on structure, change tends to seem like crisis — or to put it another way, when your idea of a system is more or less a closed system, the claustrophobia or just the boredom makes you need to burn it down periodically.

Poststructuralism is a rough name for much of the cultural theory of the last third of the 20th century. If structuralism is about space, poststructuralism is all about time, as suggested by the name. I say "*all* about time" for a reason. This does not mean thinking about structures as essentially spatial entities that also have a temporal dimension, as structures that change and grow and evolve and decay through time. It's more radical than that. It means learning to think of structures *as* events, of translating everything that seems like a structure into its *eventness*.

For example, to revisit the example raised earlier in this book, we often think of the human body as a kind of building, a large container with an inside and an outside, the me and the not-me, divided by a boundary at the skin, with nine or ten highly policed entrances and exits, not counting the pores of the skin and the belly-button (I'm not sure I've gotten this right — please check and see how many you have. Are you counting the eyes?). Of course the process, that is to say the *event* of play and negotiation between the me and the not-me — the making of the me from the not-me, the deterioration of the me into the not-me, the expulsion of the not-me, and so on — happens throughout the body. It happens not just via breathing and digestion and excretion but even more intimately in the immune system, spread throughout the body. The interplay of the me and the not-me goes on fractally, at all scales from the macro to the subatomic. The boundary is not at the skin. It is being negotiated everywhere, in every cell. The body *is* this event, this boundary traffic. And texts and cultures are like this too.

An open system, a self-making or autopoietic system, is a system that makes its own components. Language, made of sounds and letters and words — and living things, made of cells and DNA and so on — are obvious examples of systems that make their own components. It is language that carves out the infinite continuum of sounds and shapes to put together the spoken and written words out of which language is made. It's a paradox: how can a system make its own components if it has to be in existence in order to make them? But how could it be in existence if it has not yet made its components?

Why do people treat as such a puzzle the question of which came first, the chicken or the egg? It is so obvious that there were eggs long before there were chickens. Thinking in an evolutionary sense closes down some questions but it opens up others.

Why do people act as if nonlinear time were some kind of groovy, new-age concept? Time is *by definition* nonlinear — a line has one dimension, a plane two and space three, but time is recognized as a fourth dimension distinct from the three dimensions of space. One does not equal four. So-called linear time is not time at all. Let me put this another way: that which can be graphed out into a trajectory is not time. A trajectory is a *structure*.

You see a story with rising action, a crisis and a climax, followed by falling action? Go away, you're a structuralist! Try to tell me instead what happens *as* the action is rising and falling — what's going on — yeah, what's going on? But, you protest, the rising and falling *is* what happens. And again I say, go away, and come back when you're ready. Time is being at risk, the moment is a window of vulnerability. It's not about the trajectory!

Here are some little stories of trajectories.

Up: laboriously we sweated and struggled to get the sofa up four twisting flights of stairs, but when we got there, it wouldn't get through the door, and we had to bring it back down again.

Down: on the other hand, I've been to some of the lower rungs of various hells. My family took me there, my colleagues took me there, Iona and I have been there, and I've been there alone, and each time I groped around and found a little door, came up the back way and emerged again to see the stars. I think some of my old colleagues are still down there.

Why do people say that what is immediate is most alive, when it is so obvious that what is most alive requires the most complex layers and loops of mediation, the exquisite rigging, the nerves and synapses?

It is only the relation of what is happening now to what has happened and what may happen — its sameness and its difference, its constellationality with other events — that is to say, its meaning — that makes it experienceable at all!

When I try to imagine a real one-off event, something unconnected to any web of meanings stretched across past and future, I picture myself in the kitchen cooking spaghetti, head bent over pots and pans, when all of a sudden with no warning, not even a whistling noise or a bright light, at least not any that I notice, immersed as I am in making the spaghetti — BLAM! A giant meteor slams into me at a million miles an hour, and the moment when the meteor becomes a meteorite, the moment of my death, which I cannot even be said fully to experience — now *that* seems like a real, immediate present moment!

Those who remain alive will have to pick up the pieces, literally and figuratively, the latter being the easier task in this case, to try to make some meaning of it, or to come to terms with its lack of meaning (also a form of meaning-making), to knit back together their worlds without me or my spaghetti. The universe will go on with its meaning-making, its constellating of events.

Still knitting!

I'm willing to admit that my allergy to stories is a defensive one. If you wanted to tell a story about it, you could say that my childhood made me allergic to stories — that I learned to take refuge in storilessness from the traumatic and tragic story of my family, lest it pull me into its vortex. I know this is right, because it feels dangerous for me to say it. It is dangerous to give up a defense on which you have depended. But it still isn't a story. My thinking it and saying it actually leverages me into a slightly different relation to stories and storilessness. I become a different person in the process. I am reconstellated.

But, you keep repeating, isn't this a story? Isn't a story precisely a constellation and reconstellation of events? My generous answer is this: if, unlike me, you're a story person, you can keep translating everything I say into a story. But a constellation, even a constellation of events, is something more like a vision: something you see all at once, not something that unfolds in time. This is what I am going to call a *figure*.

Since I've been generous enough to allow you to re-narrativize everything if you want, are you also willing to admit, with me, that everything can just as well be cast (or miscast, if you're a glass-half-empty type) as a timeless and non-narrative figure, depending on your cognitive style?

If so, then where are we and who are we when we contemplate stories and storilessness from a third place, which is presumably neither, as we must be doing now?

Well, where are we and who are we now, when we are here together?

IV. Road Trip #3: An Answer For Thad

To get around this problem, physicists take a "cut-off" of the multiverse, cutting out a finite patch of space-time and counting the universes in it to get a representative sample. . . . This leads to incorrect probabilities of experimental outcomes in the multiverse — unless, Freivogel and his team argue, the mathematical cut-offs somehow have real and dire consequences for the places they intersect. Time would end there, they say, causing everything present to disappear. . . . The trouble began last year, with a thought experiment raised over breakfast at a conference . . . . (*New Scientist*)

While she poured him another glass of tea, he put on his

spectacles and re-examined with pleasure the luminous yellow, green, red little jars. His clumsy moist lips spelled out their eloquent labels: apricot, grape, beech plum, quince. He had got to crab apple, when the telephone rang again. (Vladimir Nabokov, "Symbols and Signs")

i.

At a beginning-of-the-year party, I joined a small group of faculty who were gathered around Thad Ziolkowski, the head of Pratt Institute's creative writing program. He was talking about Swiss psychoanalyst Carl Jung and Jung's quasi-mystical account of *synchronicity*. When I joined them, Thad was in the middle of telling how Jung had been visiting a small town where his host served him plum cake — the first time he'd ever had it — and how, twenty years later, Jung chanced to return to the same town, stopped in a café and was charmed to find plum cake on the menu. He hadn't eaten it again in the twenty-year interval, so when the waiter came over, he ordered it, but the waiter said, "I'm sorry sir; the last piece was just ordered by *this gentleman here*," and who should he point out but the very same man who had served Jung the plum cake twenty years earlier!

I told Thad it was weird that he should be telling this story, since I had just written a chapter called "Signs and Miracles," which was dedicated to figuring out the logic of exactly these kinds of uncanny incidents. Long ago I had read Jung's autobiography, and though I didn't recall the plum cake story, I did remember a similar one. After a day that included several incidents involving fish, Jung came home to find that — lo and behold — "there was fish for dinner." What struck me was the phrasing, "there was fish," as if the fish magically appeared on  the table, as if the fact that his wife or his servants planned and cooked the meal were irrelevant — and it occurred to me that some of how the incident struck him must have had to do with how thoroughly removed he was from mundane things like meal preparation.

Thad appreciated this observation but worried that maybe I was trying to reduce the mystical part of synchronicity down to some kind of misrecognition of the network of labor and gender relations from which it emerged. I assured him that the aim of my analysis was to dig deeper, through reason and demystification, and back into the miraculous again.

He put me on the spot and asked me how I would explain the plum cake incident. I said a few things, but I didn't have a satisfying answer. I knew his question would stay simmering in my brain until I got back to it.

ii.

The next day, Friday, I made the hour-and-a-half hour drive from Brooklyn to eastern Long Island to see Iona, who teaches there, at Stony Brook University, where I had also taught for seventeen years. For the last twelve of those years, I'd commuted by car from my apartment in Brooklyn, so three years before, when I started teaching at Pratt Institute — a twenty-minute walk from my apartment — I found I actually missed the commute, which had always served as a contemplative time for me; my car was a little meditation room on wheels. I had gotten so conditioned by it that sometimes I still need a long car trip to open up a space to rethink and reorient myself.

Sure enough, as soon as I got in the car and started on my way, I began to think about the plum cake incident again.

Would it matter (I wondered) if it turned out that Jung's host had plum cake every day in the same café at the same time, and that they always saved the last piece for him? After all, Jung was Swiss, wasn't he? And aren't the Swiss known for the clockwork regularity of their habits? Or what if the town was Pflaumenkuchenburg and Jung happened to visit on the final day of their annual festival, and the waiter had gone on to offer him fresh plums, or plum ice cream, or maybe some delicious plum liqueur?

But then my brain veered off into another story, one I had heard my grandmother tell more than once. She was visiting us sometime when I was little, and my father — himself a scholar who had been deeply influenced by Jung — brought the famous Jungian thinker Joseph Campbell home for dinner. My grandmother made strawberry shortcake. It turned out to be the first time Campbell ever had it, and he loved it. Imagine, she'd say, this big-shot scholar who'd been all around the world, and he'd never had strawberry shortcake! Of course she loved the fact that she was the one who made it for him.

I started wondering if he might have been saying it was *as if* he'd never had it before — as in the Madonna song "Like a Virgin," where her lover fucks her so good it's *as if* it were the first time. Maybe that was just how good my grandmother had strawberry-shortcaked Campbell. Or maybe, since he must have gotten invited to lots of dinners on the lecture circuit, Campbell figured out that people loved it if he told them it was the first time he'd ever had a dish, and maybe this was not cynical on his part but actually served to enhance their pleasure as well as his own — after all, he was known for the slogan *follow your bliss*. Maybe there were lots of people out there who would swell with pride with the memory of how they were the first one to serve Campbell peach cobbler, or pot roast. After all, there has to be a first time for everything, and having been raised in a Waspy American household in the first half of the twentieth century, one with (no doubt) a very narrow cuisine, Campbell would have discovered all kinds of new dishes as he made his way in the world.

And herein lies the uncanny echo of the plum cake incident. Is there something about Jung and Jungians that their experience of fruit desserts is so impoverished? So when they do encounter such desserts, it's as if the experience were bathed in a miraculous glow?

iii.

Something else about Thad's version of the plum cake story had stuck with me: the words *this gentleman here* in the waiter's comment: "I'm sorry sir; the last piece was just ordered by *this gentleman here*." As I was ruminating about my grandmother's story, I remembered why these words seemed familiar: it was one of my old favorite jokes.

In this joke, a guy is working as a clerk in the produce department of a grocery store. A customer approaches him with a grapefruit in hand and asks if he can buy half of it. The guy says he has to check with his manager, so he goes to the back room and says to the manager, "some asshole wants to buy half of this grapefruit," but then he looks and sees that the customer is standing right behind him, so he adds, "and *this gentleman here* would like to buy the other half."

After the customer leaves, the manager tells the clerk he was impressed at how he'd handled the situation — so impressed that he wants to make the clerk a manager of his own produce department. "Unfortunately," he says, "the only openings we have are in Canada." "Canada!" the clerk exclaims: "The only people in Canada are either whores or hockey players!" The manager is outraged: "I'll have you know that my *wife* happens to be Canadian!" "Oh really," responds the clerk; "which team does she play for?"

Although it was the *this gentleman here* remark that made me think of the joke, it didn't escape my notice that, as in the plum cake and the strawberry shortcake stories, fruit also makes a key appearance in the joke.

I started thinking about how it's the clerk's smart mouth that gets him into trouble — and gets him out of trouble again. I hate to ruin a joke by explanation, but there's something very deep about this. The coincidences aren't really events in themselves — the fact that the customer turns out to have followed him into the back room, or that the manager's wife happens to be Canadian.

It's the guy's smart mouth that makes them into events.

Trouble — like meaning and the miraculous — isn't just there waiting for us to step into. It's what our own intelligence compels us continually to manufacture. It's how we're wired into the world. And this doesn't deflate the sublimity — it *is* the sublimity.

iv.

Back again to trying to explain the plum cake incident, I started mapping it out in my head as I drove. I began by imagining Jung's path in space and time through the world, and his host's path. If his host spent most of his life in the small town, his path would be a straight line, staying in one place in space as it moved forward continuously in time. If you factor in the movement of the earth and the sun, it would actually be a fractal series of spirals, but let's leave that aside for the moment. Looking even more closely at the line, you'd see all the little zigzags as the guy goes back and forth, from his house to work and to the café, day after day. You'd see his path and Jung's converging, diverging for twenty years, and then converging again in the café.

Now imagine the paths of all the plum cakes over the same space and time. They'd be lots of very short lines, since each plum cake would exist for a few days at most, and they would be likely to travel only very short distances in space during their ephemeral lives.

So the whole space-time map on which Jung and his host's wandering trajectories are traced would also be covered all over with a fine, short stubble of plum cake trajectories.

And this map is just a start. Ideally, you would have to consider various branchings of all the trajectories of the men and the cakes, since at every point there are any number of likely scenarios, and only in retrospect can we reduce them to a series of lines. The so-called *many-universes interpretation* of quantum mechanics is an attempt to recognize the continual coexistence of these many possible paths, each forking path constituting an alternate universe. If you were able to visualize the branchings, even the plum cake stubble might turn into a fractal forest or a feathered wing.

In an adjacent universe, maybe the guy serves Jung peach cobbler instead of plum cake, but everything else is the same.

In still another branching universe, maybe the guy gets waylaid on route to the café, so they think he's not coming and sell his peach cobbler to Jung, and when the guy walks in and Jung recognizes him, Jung is so surprised that he chokes and dies, but the guy goes on to write a famous account of the incident called "The Peach Cobbler Always Rings Twice."

And maybe in still another universe, it's the guy himself who is a cobbler, and Jung is not an Aryan psychoanalyst but a rabbi, and the small town is Chelm, the Village of Fools in Yiddish folktales. The rabbi leaves a pair of shoes with the cobbler to be repaired but then forgets about them until he finds the ticket in a drawer twenty years later, and when he brings the ticket into the cobbler's shop, he finds the cobbler sitting there reading the Borges short story "The Garden of Forking Paths." Whatever else happens in this timeline, you just know that cobbler will go into the back room and come back to tell the rabbi that the shoes aren't ready yet.

And maybe in still another universe, it isn't Carl Jung at all but *me*, and I'm sitting on a plane next to a German woman, and when we are served blueberry muffins, the woman eats hers with a spoon. See how we've stumbled back from the hypothetical into our actual universe again? This actually happened! And notice that again it involves someone with obviously very limited experience of certain fruit desserts. And by the way, this woman was reading not Borges but a tabloid with the headline WHITNEY'S MOM BEGS POP DIVA TO GET HELP (still several years before Whitney Houston's death at age forty-eight). She stared at the headline for something like half an hour, leading me to speculate that her English was limited and she was laboriously trying to work out what it all meant. In any case, the proximity of the words MOM and POP in the headline might have been confusing to her.

v.

I'm now about two-thirds of the way to Stony Brook, and my alternate-universes reverie is interrupted by the realization that it is here — at this precise spot on Highway 347 but on the other side of the wide, tree-and-grass-covered median — that a strange incident occurred about five years earlier.

The political philosopher Michael Hardt — one of my old editors — had come to speak at Stony Brook, and after he had done so, I drove him to the city. Traffic slowed to a crawl, and we approached a place where a bunch of police cars were parked at various angles on the grass of the median, some with their lights flashing, and as we passed them, a cop was emphatically waving traffic along and repeating, *"Don't look at it! Just keep moving! Don't look at it!"* We couldn't even see what *it* might have been — there didn't seem to be any kind of accident. Maybe it was just the cop's way of saying *move along, nothing to see here*, but it certainly made everything seem creepy.

The following week I was talking with some graduate students about Hardt's visit and I mentioned this incident, whereupon one student told me excitedly that she had also driven into the city after class and had passed the same scene, which had led her to search the internet for some reference to this major police activity. What she found was that, apparently, someone had deposited a trunk with human body parts in it, and that it was probably connected with some serial killings on Long Island. Of course I was shocked by this, and later I searched the internet myself for any mention of the incident but couldn't find any. When I asked the student, she said she had also looked again but came up with nothing the second time around, so she could only assume that the police, not wanting to compromise an ongoing investigation, had ensured that all leaked references to it were quickly removed.

A couple of years later, I ran into Michael at an academic conference and asked him if he remembered the incident. He didn't, but having brought it up, I felt compelled to tell him the rest of the story. Halfway through, he said "wow, that's amazing" or words to that effect, and a funny smile passed across his face.

When I'd finished telling the story, he said he'd remembered something else about our trip after all, something so compelling it must have washed away any other memories: that Iona had visited some farm on the eastern end of Long Island — an operation the workers had managed to take over and were running themselves — and that she had sent us off with a bag of just-picked peaches, and that the most ethereal aroma had filled the car all the way to Brooklyn. It had made him think of the Chinese legends of divine peaches that confer immortality, or maybe it was Iona who'd suggested this to him.

You've got to hand it to Michael: he had managed to remember the divine glow — *and* the network of labor and gender relations from which it emerged!

vi.

> Wind and helmsman held us on our course,
> and I'd have reached my native land unharmed,
> but North Wind, sea currents, and the waves
> pushed me off course, as I was doubling back around . . .
> (Homer, *The Odyssey*)

I thought I'd better not show up at Iona's empty-handed, so I stopped at the Rolling Pin Bakery, and I was charmed to see that they had plum cake!

On Sunday I drove back to Brooklyn. As I approached the stretch of road where the *"Don't look at it"* incident had occurred,

I started looking for the exact spot where it had happened — the spot I had been so sure of when I had passed it going the other way. But now that I was on the side of the road where it had happened, all the scrub trees and grass looked pretty much the same, just as one line of text looks like every other. Maybe there were serial killers lurking in these suburban woods and bodies buried all over, who knows. But however many trunks full of

 body parts had ever been deposited here, or whatever mystical revelations or peach-induced trances had ever been experienced by people driving by, the trees and the grass and the asphalt weren't saying.

I thought of the lines from Allen Ginsberg's poem *Howl*:

> Visions! omens! hallucinations! miracles! ecstasies! gone
> down the American river!
> Breakthroughs! over the river! flips and crucifixions! gone
> down the flood!

This made me want to turn to you, Thad, and to speak up in defiance of such a somber truth, as if you were somehow the one trying to rain on my parade. But even as I struggled against it, I found myself being pulled deeper. I wanted to say something about how we can be so smart and so stupid at the same time, and how, even when everything seems uneventful, as in this story, floating down a lazy river, we are getting ourselves into more trouble than we can imagine, every moment we're alive — *is that the sound of the waterfall getting louder? and now the smell of the spray?* — and how our greatest and also most lamentable achievement — and maybe the most remarkable fact of the architecture of complex systems — is that we're not consumed more quickly by the continual maelstrom of miracles and signs and synchronicities out of which our minds and our worlds are woven.

vii.

A while back, when I was looking for something on the internet, I stumbled by chance on an account of the Japanese Buddhist monks — known as *sokushinbutsu* — who cause their own deaths in such a way as to result in their mummification.

Of many hundreds who tried, mostly in previous centuries, only about twenty have been found. Here's how they did it: for a thousand days the monk would eat only nuts and seeds and follow a rigorous exercise regimen, to burn off all body fat. Then for another thousand days he would eat only bark and roots, and begin drinking poison tea made with the sap of the Urushi tree, from which lacquer is made. This purged the body of fluids and would help keep the maggots away. When the end was near, the monk would entomb himself in a tiny underground room only big enough to sit up in. An air shaft allowed him to keep breathing, and he would ring a bell periodically to indicate he was still alive. After the bell stopped, the monks would seal the air shaft and wait another thousand days before opening it to see if the mummification had worked. If it had, the monk was proclaimed a Buddha and put on view. More often than not, though, they found a decomposed body — evidence of extreme dedication, but not buddhahood.

I hate suicide. The intensity of my abhorrence comes from the fact that my own father — the Jungian scholar I mentioned earlier — killed himself when I was a child, and it still seems to me that suicide violates the social contract. Maybe someone who commits suicide is in unbearable psychological pain, but when you violate a bond so fundamental (it seems to me) you forfeit any tears of pity that might have been shed on your behalf, not to mention buddhahood. I still love my father, and his capacity for love and joy is the still-beating heart of his legacy to me. But the condemnation of suicide is still so much at the core of my personality that, when reading about the *sokushinbutsu* evoked in me something more like awe and respect, it felt disorienting, like looking over the edge of a bottomless pit. I could feel a buzzing numbness around my face, as if I had drunk the poison tea myself.

It's true that the monks were not abandoning children, and they were acting with the encouragement of their fellows, but even more than this, there was something about the meticulous slowness of their preparation that made what they were doing something other than suicide, and that's what had gotten through my radar. Later I realized that this must be because, as I have read somewhere, suicide often comes down to more a matter of impulse control than of longterm depression, and this is why — counter to what you might expect — many people who are saved from suicide at the last moment don't go back and try again. I've heard that, in Catholicism, there can be forgiveness for suicide because there is always the possibility that, in a final moment — say, after the jump but before the rope snaps taut — there was regret and repentance: an escape hatch inside an escape hatch. You've got to admit, that's a pretty poignant piece of casuistry.

Anyway, so it happened that day, driving back from Iona's house, and after having been unable to pinpoint the place where the *don't-look-at-it* incident had happened, and thinking of all the synchronicities and miracles lost, and buried in my thoughts, I suddenly felt my car was the monk's little room only big enough to sit up in, and I felt — this time not just in my face but across the entire space-time trajectory of my life — an identification with the *sokushinbutsu*.

The writer buries himself in his text, alive for a little while, but many of those who come to the text will come after he has stopped ringing the bell, and if he's lucky, what they find will be desiccated but intact.

Just as life is sweet because touched by death, so death reverberates with echoes of life — thanks to those who carry a tinkling bell to the threshold of the void — and is claimed for life by those who sit sipping tea on its vast and melancholy shores.

viii.

When I got back to my apartment building, the lady in 5J had printed out a note and taped it to the elevator door, as she often does when things go wrong in the building. This time the note was titled "Horror of Horrors" and it told how someone had thrown something smoldering into the trash compactor, but whatever it was had been found and put out before any harm was done. On seeing this note, it struck me that the trash compactor sits in a small underground room — in the basement, connected to the upper floors via a shaft — just like a *sokushin-butsu* in his buddha-hole. What made me laugh was how the note said that "someone was a little careless in disposing of something not yet extinguished."

I took this as a sign that the reign of the Unexpected Fruits was over, and that the Self-Mummifying Monks had gained at least a temporary foothold.

ix.

> Mona Lisa must have had the highway blues; you can tell by the way she smiles. (Bob Dylan)

I wrote the above account immediately upon returning to my apartment — just banged it out that evening, very unlike my usually much slower writing practice — and though I revised it repeatedly over the next few months, it didn't change much.

At one point, I added (and later removed) an Author's Note: "When I used to read this essay aloud to an audience, *when I was alive*, I rang a little bell between the sections."

This note seemed to me to enact what turns out to be a central point of the essay. Admittedly, the dead are usually not allowed to speak of themselves as dead, except in certain genres like horror movies and religion. But on the other hand, after an author dies, (1) do all the "I" statements in his writing become false, since their referent no longer exists, or (2) is the author a kind of twilight figure in the first place, neither or both alive or dead? (Hint: *it's number two*.) In any case, my Author's Note would have been a classic instance of the rhetorical figure of speech known as *prolepsis*: "the representation or assumption of a future act or development as being presently existing or accomplished." But my friend Alex, a fiction writer, advised me to remove the note since it induced the reader to expect that the narrator would die in the course of the story to follow. Not being a fiction writer myself, I hadn't thought of that, but I had to admit she was right. The narrator wasn't going to die *in the story*. It was I who had been going to die *in real time*. (Please notice that, unless you take the last sentence to mean that I had been going to die but somehow dodged the bullet, it implies that I have since, in fact, died. So you see I snuck the prolepsis back in after all.)

I did read the piece to an audience, about a month after writing it, and I did ring a little bell between the sections: *still alive!*

About a week after performing the essay, I was again driving out to Port Jefferson to see Iona and again musing about the events of the essay and the essay itself, when something struck me about it.

When I say *struck me*, I mean *like a bolt of lightning*.

Being struck by lightning changes people. Sometimes it kills them outright. Sometimes they have to learn again to speak and walk. Sometimes they feel as if they've lost something, but they just can't put a name on it. If they could, they probably wouldn't have lost it. (I once drove past a sign that said *Hidden Driveway* and I thought: *but I don't see any hidden driveway.* And then I thought: *Exactly.*) Sometimes people who've been struck by lightning feel as if they've gained something, but they can't say what it is. Little things are different: they find themselves finishing other people's sentences, or they find themselves noticing what they do with their hands when they're nervous. If you connect up all the little things, maybe they form a constellation, like being reborn under a new sign of the zodiac. Sometimes you change, but you don't know that you've changed. And of course you don't have to be struck by lightning to change: it can be slower, like living under a high-voltage power line; a neurological disorder no doctor can detect, because it's fifty feet overhead. But don't try telling anyone that the Consolidated Edison Company has been rewiring your brain and your voice and your hands by remote control while you sleep!

Anyway, what struck me in the car felt that melodramatic to me. It dawned on me both slowly and quickly, and when the realization washed over me, I actually had to swerve back into my lane.

Dear Reader, can you guess what it was that struck me?

You should know, since it has been staring you in the face the whole time. I might even say that, at some level anyway, *you do know*, even if you don't know that you know.

What struck me was that I had experienced the real-time events of the essay — that is, the drive to Port Jefferson and back, and all of what I had been thinking about — including all the stuff about my father, death, road trips, signs and miracles, and so on — and that I had written and later performed the essay — *all without mentioning or even thinking about Professor Lee — not even once.*

It struck me as *shame* strikes — the sudden flush that is both cold and hot: how *could* you? In the ground for so little time, and already forgotten?

Almost immediately I had a defensive reaction, which was the realization that Professor Lee had conspired to make his own effacement happen, by insisting that that I use the fake name and that no particular facts about him be mentioned — and, on top of that, just by dying (damn him!). Accordingly, I had gotten used to writing about the things we talked about without mentioning him at all — in fact, I had to go out of my way to try to reconstruct our early conversations in the beginning of this book, avoiding anything revealing about his identity. So on one hand, there was my experience of him, full of personal data and details and memories from our time together, and on the other, the almost completely abstracted and impersonalized figure — the *cypher* — to which he had insisted I reduce him in this writing. Is it any wonder that my own otherwise replete experience of him would begin to be pulled into the orbit of the cypher?

But even as I recognized the validity of this reaction, I knew full well that what happened was *not* that I'd forgotten Professor Lee and then felt a pang of guilt about it. In any case, guilt is about things one had a choice about doing or not doing, while shame is about one's *identity* — and the commission or omission of only those actions that follow from *who one is*.

Just as finding Professor Lee again had changed me, the loss of him had left its mark too. Notice how, in the essay, everything is going along happily until the melancholy turn to all the stuff about loss, the *sokushinbutsu*, and my father. The melancholy turn seems to come from nowhere — unless you realize that it must be the marker of something unsaid, an absence that can't even be spoken but makes itself felt — a kind of ghost. No surprise that Professor Lee would haunt my meditations on the sublime, skulking at one remove from what's explicit in the text.

Isn't the idea that ghosts hang around because of some unfinished business?

I always knew that my relationship with Professor Lee was, at some level, a way for me come to terms with my father and his suicide. The Professor and I had talked about this openly. He wasn't exactly a father figure, but because he and my father had been close friends, and because (like my father) he was so kind — but (unlike my father) not wracked by self-hatred and despondency — my connection with him and even my coming to terms with his death had worked to soften the scars of that old wound. In other words, my relationship with him was a safer space for

me to replay and revise the old trauma. And behind it all —
behind Professor Lee and my father and the loss of them both —
lie the pangs of coming to terms with that which at some level
one cannot come to terms with at all, the dark side of the
sublime, the parts of our lost love objects we have incorporated
into ourselves, the weave of ourselves we owe to others but
could never acknowledge without unraveling, without ceasing
to be ourselves.

And yet we do unravel. We are lightning-struck, and we
change.

I thought of another old professor of mine from grad school,
Diane Middlebrook. Occasionally, when responding to
something I had written, she would use the word *wonderful*.
There was such an emphatic lilt and warmth in the way she said
it, but there was something distant about it too — the distance of
aesthetic appreciation. I was gratified by the praise and kindness
directed at me, but strange to say, I primarily identified *with her*
at that moment. I can hear her saying the word and feel the
resonance of it in me. I want to say that *the resonance of this one
word in me was how I learned to be a teacher*, to approach my
students by looking for what's alive in their writing, to be ready
to be engaged by it and to engage it with them. The shorthand
version is that I downloaded the core of my teaching persona
from Diane. She died of cancer in 2007, at age sixty-eight.

I thought back on how Professor Lee had smiled, in our first
meeting in the nursing home, and how I knew then that he was
smiling at the thought that, because of his injunction against me
mentioning any personal information about him, readers would
always suspect that he was just an invented alter ego of mine.

As sure as I had been at the time that I recognized exactly
what had made him smile, another dimension of his smile now
opened up to me. No matter whether or not he knew of his
terminal illness at that moment — no matter how quickly at his
back he was hearing "time's winged chariot hurrying near" — he

must also have smiled in the recognition that, if and when I wrote the book we were talking about, *he would probably be gone*, and thus would be reduced by the book to something like an alter ego of mine after all — reduced to whatever of him I would have metabolized, whatever ghost of him I had managed to download into my brain and my text.

And who knows, maybe in that moment he also saw me *not* seeing this, or imagined that I would come to understand it only later, in the wake of his death — or only, as it now has happened, in the process of my letting go of him. In any case, my new take on the moment could only happen as a result of me thinking with some new bemusement about how *my own writing would outlive me*. I had to smile this smile myself before recognizing it in him.

And that was the moment I so confidently labeled with his term *recognition to infinity*! In fact, it was a much more complicated transaction involving significant *misrecognition*, reciprocal but always asymmetrical, never finished — a strange attractor. I now understood in Professor Lee's smile something rueful or poignant — the recognition that he would be gone (and maybe even his recognition of my blithe non-recognition of this) — as well as something mischievous (his delight at conspiring in his own effacement, or just the way a master invents diabolical challenges for his disciple) and something loving (his happiness that I would go on living, and maybe that something of him would go on living in me as well).

I can't say how much of the recognitions and misrecognitions of that moment I may only have imagined, but I do know that the *circuit* of that smile between us continues to lighten and enlighten me.

It's alive!

Yes, the playful and the melancholic views of language are opposed, but only like muscle groups that pull in different directions to shape this smile.

I thought of that enigmatic little poem of William Blake:

There is a smile of love,
And there is a smile of deceit,
And there is a smile of smiles
In which these two smiles meet.

And there is a frown of hate,
And there is a frown of disdain,
And there is a frown of frowns
Which you strive to forget in vain;

For it sticks in the heart's deep core,
And it sticks in the deep back bone.
And no smile that ever was smil'd
But only one smile alone,

That betwixt the cradle & grave
It only once smil'd can be;
But when it once is smil'd,
There's an end to all misery.

Acknowledgements

This book is dedicated to all my teachers.

Thanks to Terrence Deacon for permission to use the diagram from his astounding book *The Symbolic Species* (Norton, 1997). All other illustrations are photos by the author and friends; cover art by the author. Thanks to Danielle Skorzanka for cover design and all-around righteousness; to Bruno Clarke for ongoing support and advice; to Alexandra Chasin for big help with Chapter One and big love always; to Lol Fow for additional editing; to my great colleagues, friends and students at Pratt Institute; to my graduate students from Stony Brook — and above all to Iona, my other I. Thanks also to many other friends and loved ones who appear in one form or another in these pages, or who have provided particular inspiration and support along the way: Roger Blakely, Zoa Chasin, Ann Christensen, Ed Cohen, Leonard Cohen, Nicolas Crook, George Cunningham, Maria Damon, Judith Halberstam, Michael Hardt, Gillian Johns, David Kazanjian, Jim Keller, Ray and Claire Livingston, Maggie Livingston, Sarah Livingston, Kelly Mays, Diane Middlebrook, Ira and Josephine Rubel, Josie Saldana, Clayton Sankey, Gray Sansom-Chasin, Clio and Isabella Walsh, Lang Walsh, Liam Walsh, and Thad Ziolkowski. Please see additional acknowledgements and credits in the references section, below.

References

Introduction: The Vision of Ezekiel and the Films of Stanley Kubrick

"Reflection does not withdraw": Maurice Merleau-Ponty, *The Phenomenology of Perception* (London: Routledge, 2002), xv.

"Most of the time, an electron": Stephen Battersby, "The Flash" in *New Scientist*, Vol. 211, No. 2831 (Sept. 24, 2011), 46-49, p. 47.

"Terrence Deacon's book": *The Symbolic Species: The Co-evolution of Language and the Brain* (New York: Norton, 1997). The account of the emergence of the symbolic referenced here is on pp. 69-101; the diagram appears on page 87.

"the little wheel runs by faith": Woody Guthrie, "Ezekiel Saw the Wheel," *Woody Guthrie: The Early Years*, Essential Media Group, 2008.

"Smail offers a single explanation": Daniel Lord Smail, *On Deep History and the Brain* (Berkeley: University of California Press, 2008).

"the FreeCell habit started": this and the quote that follows are from Ellen Kaye, "One Down, 31,999 to Go: Surrendering to a Solitary Obsession," *New York Times*, October 17, 2002.

"the anticipation of a meeting": Andre Green, *Le Discours Vivant*, 1973.

"unties knots in our thinking": Ludwig Wittgenstein, in *The Wittgenstein Reader*, ed. Anthony Kenny (Oxford: Blackwell, 1994), 272.

"the band in heaven": Talking Heads, "Heaven," from *Fear of Music* (recording), Sire Records, 1979.

"Wordsworth complained": all quotes are from William Wordsworth's "Preface" to *Lyrical Ballads* (1800), in *English Romantic Writers*, ed. David Perkins (San Diego: Harcourt Brace Jovanovich, 1967), 320-331.

185

"Samuel Taylor Coleridge considered artists": S.T. Coleridge, *On the Constitution of Church and State*, ed. John Colmer (London and Princeton, NJ: Princeton University Press); *The Collected Works of Samuel Taylor Coleridge*, Vol. X., 46.

"Hulme defined Romanticism": "T. E. Hulme, "Romanticism and Classicism," in Robert Gleckner and Gerald Ensoe, eds., *Romanticism: Points of View*, 2nd Ed., 55-65 (Detroit: Wayne State University Press, 1975), 58.

"the great danger with which fiction threatens the world": Michel Foucault, "What Is an Author" in *The Foucault Reader*, ed. Paul Rabinow, 101-20 (New York: Pantheon Books, 1984), 118.

Chapter One: Miracles and Signs

"we simultaneously both *find* and *invent* the world": see D. W. Winnicot, *Playing and Reality* (Routledge, 1989), 89.

"Perhaps kindling in the amygdala": V.S. Ramachandran, *Phantoms in the Brain* (New York: HarperCollins, 1998), 251.

"Theoretical physics . . . is fiction": Giovanni Vignale, "The power of the abstract"; *New Scientist*, Feb. 26, 2011; 32-35 (32).

W. B. Yeats and the fairies: cited in Dipesh Chakrabarty, *Provincializing Europe*, (Princeton U. Press, 2000), 111.

"The Emmet's Inch & Eagle's Mile": William Blake, "Auguries of Innocence," in *The Complete Poetry and Prose*, new rev. ed., ed. David Erdman (Garden City, N.Y.: Doubleday, Anchor Press).

"Energy is the only life": William Blake, from "The Marriage of Heaven and Hell," in *The Complete Poetry and Prose*, new rev. ed., ed. David Erdman (Garden City, N.Y.: Doubleday, Anchor Press).

Christina Aguilera, "Fighter," from *Stripped* (audio CD; RCA, 2002).

"I'm just like that bird": Bob Dylan, "You're a Big Girl Now," from *Blood on the Tracks*, (Columbia, 1984).

"system-as-juggling": see Ira Livingston, *Between Science and Literature: An Introduction to Autopoetics* (Illinois U. Press,

2006), 84.

"the love that moves the sun and other stars": Dante, *The Divine Comedy* 3: *Paradiso*, transl. John D. Sinclair (Oxford U. Press, 1939).

"As Captain Reynolds said": from the film *Serenity*, written and directed by Joss Wheedon (Universal, 2005).

"sheaf of times": actually it was Michel Serres, in "The Origin of Language: Biology, Information Theory, & Thermodynamics" from *Hermes; Literature, Science, Philosophy*, ed. Josue V. Harari and David F. Bell (Baltimore: Johns Hopkins University Press, 1982), 10.

"The Old Cumberland Beggar": in William Wordsworth, *Poetical Works*, ed. Thomas Hutchinson and rev. Ernest de Selincourt (Oxford U. Press, 1969).

Arrow of Chaos: Ira Livingston, *Arrow of Chaos: Romanticism and Postmodernity* (University of Minnesota Press, 1997).

"across the highways of America in tears": Allen Ginsberg, *Howl and Other Poems* (San Francisco: City Lights, 1956).

"and we rose again to see the stars": Dante, *The Divine Comedy* 1: *Inferno*, transl. John D. Sinclair (Oxford U. Press, 1939), 427.

"many a quaint and curious volume of forgotten lore": Edgar Allan Poe, "The Raven."

"Stay, illusion!": from William Shakspeare, *Hamlet*, Act One, Scene One, lines 127-128.

"something beyond which we cannot go": Wittgenstein, in *The Wittgenstein Reader*. Ed. Anthony Kenny. Oxford; Blackwell, 1994; 276.

"When the Creator told Noah": cited in Rav P. S. Berg, The Essential Zohar. New York: Bell Tower [Random House], 2002; 137.

"Then I came back to where I'd been": Leonard Cohen, "Love Itself," from *Ten New Songs* (audio CD), Sony 2001.

"Time is peculiarly chopped up": Marcel Proust, cited in Walter Benjamin, "On Some Motifs in Baudelaire," in *Poetry and*

Cultural Studies: A Reader, ed. Maria Damon and Ira Livingston (Urbana, IL: University of Illinois Press, 2009, 37-55), 50.

Percy Shelley, "Mont Blanc," in *Shelley's Poetry and Prose,* ed. Donald Reiman (Norton, 1977), 89-93.

Samuel T. Coleridge, "Kubla Khan," in *Samuel Taylor Coleridge* (Oxford Authors series), ed. H.J. Jackson (Oxford U. Press).

"day and night with such fervor": from Juliet Bredon, *Peking: A Historical and Intimate Description of Its Chief Places of Interest* (3rd ed. Shanghai: Kelly & Walsh, Ltd. 1931), cited in Morris Rossabi, *Khubilai Khan: His Life and Times* (Berkeley: University of California Press, 1988).

"identical-twin flamenco guitarists": I have since learned that the guitarists were Guillermo and Gabriel Ariza, a duo known as Gimaguas.

"a Keats letter from 1819": *Letters of John Keats,* ed. Robert Gittings (Oxford U. Press, 1970), 229-230.

"sometimes known as the Great Chain of Being": see Arthur O. Lovejoy, *The Great Chain of Being: A Study of the History of an Idea* (Cambridge, Massachusetts: Harvard University Press, 1936).

"expected emergent collective property": Stuart Kauffman, *The Origins of Order: Self-Organization and Selection in Evolution* (New York: Oxford University Press, 1993), xvi.

"climbing Mount Improbable": see Richard Dawkins, *Climbing Mount Improbable* (Norton, 1997).

"our sense of a 'present moment'": see Daniel Stern, *The Present Moment in Psychotherapy and Everyday Life* (Norton, 2004).

"window of simultaneity": Francisco Varela, in "The Specious Present: A Neurophenomenology of Time Consciousness," in *Naturalizing Phenomenology,* ed. Jean Petitot, Varela et al, 266-312 (Stanford U. Press, 1999), cited in Patricia Clough, "The Affective Turn," in *The Affect Theory Reader,* ed. Melissa Gregg and Gregory J. Seligworth, Duke U. Press, 2010; 206-225), 213.

Chapter Two: Beginnings

"Not chess, Mr. Spock: *poker*": from "The Corbomite Maneuver" episode of *Star Trek* original TV series.

Murray Gell-Mann on "frozen accidents": Murray Gell-Mann, "What is complexity?" in *Complexity* Vol. 1, Issue 1 (1995), 16-19.

"If it were not for this swerve": Lucretius, *On the Nature of Things*, transl. W.E. Leonard, Book II (Internet Classics Archive, http://classics.mit.edu//Carus/nature_things.html).

Morowitz on frozen accidents: Harold J. Morowitz, *The Emergence of Everything: How the World Became Complex* (Oxford U. Press, 2002), 23.

"the designs found in nature are nothing short of brilliant": Daniel C. Dennett, "Intelligent design? Show me the science," in the *New York Times*, August 29, 2005.

"people named Dennis": from "Why Susie Sells Seashells by the Seashore: Implicit Egotism and Major Life Decisions" by Brett W. Pelham, Matthew C. Mirenberg, and John T. Jones, *Journal of Personality and Social Psychology*, 2002, Vol. 82, No. 4, 469–487), 480.

"a paper on allergic airways inflammation": cited in *New Scientist* Vol. 206, No. 2764; 12 June 2010, 56.

"full of fine things said unintentionally": *Letters of John Keats*, ed. Robert Gittings (Oxford U. Press, 1970), 40.

"not through the boardroom": A.G. Cairns-Smith, *Seven Clues to the Origin of Life* (Cambridge U. Press, 1985), 53.

"a complex collaboration": Cairns-Smith, *Seven Clues* (58).

"an arch of stones": Cairns-Smith, *Seven Clues*, 59-60.

"the urgent need to communicate": D. W. Winnicot, *The Maturational Processes and the Facilitating Environment* (Karnac Books, 1996), 185.

"the author function": Michel Foucault, "What is an Author," in *The Foucault Reader*, ed. Paul Rabinow (New York: Pantheon Books, 1985), 101-120.

"the sudden awareness that everything is alive": William Burroughs, "Apocalypse," on *Dead City Radio* (CD; New York: Island Records, 1990).

Chapter Three: Getting Stuck and Unstuck

"I long ago lost a hound": Henry David Thoreau, *Walden*, in *Walden and Resistance to Civil Government*, ed. William Rossi (Norton, 1992), 8.

"oceanic feeling": Sigmund Freud, *Civilization and its Discontents*, transl./ed. James Strachey (Norton, 1961), 11-12.

"the sense of darkness coming over me": Keats letter to Charles Brown, 9/30/1820, in *Letters of John Keats*, ed. Robert Gittings (Oxford U. Press, 1970), 394.

"Freud watched his infant grandson": Sigmund Freud, *Beyond the Pleasure Principle*, transl./ed. James Strachey (Norton, 1961), 8-10.

"I can scarcely bid you good-bye": *Letters of John Keats*, ed. Robert Gittings (Oxford U. Press, 1970), 399.

"at my back I always hear": Andrew Marvell, "To His Coy Mistress," in *The Complete Poems*, ed. Elizabeth Story Donno (Penguin, 1972), 50.

"Benjamin's famous Angel of History" and subsequent quotes: Walter Benjamin, "Theses on the Philosophy of History," in *Illuminations*, ed./intro. Hannah Arendt, transl. Harry Zohn (Harcourt Brace Jovanvich/Schocken, 1969), 253-264.

"Edwin Abbot's famous 1884 novella": *Flatland: A Romance of Many Dimensions*, (Oxford, 2008).

"time nexus": Frank Herbert, *Dune* (Ace Books, 1987), 296.

"somewhere ahead of him": *Dune*, 317.

Leonard Mlodinow, *The Drunkard's Walk* (Random House/ Vintage, 2009), 104-05.

"when you have eliminated the impossible": Arthur Conan Doyle, from "The Sign of the Four"; *The Complete Sherlock Holmes* (Doubleday, 1970), 111.

"animism of everyday life": Alan J. Fridlund, "The Behavioral Ecology View of Smiling and Other Facial Expressions," in *An Empirical Reflection on the Smile*, ed. Millicent H. Abel; Lewiston, NY: Edwin Mellen Press, 2002, pp 45-82, 72.

"a God who 'only Acts and Is in existing beings'": William Blake, from "The Marriage of Heaven and Hell," in *The Complete Poetry and Prose*, new rev. ed., ed. David Erdman (Garden City, N.Y.: Doubleday, Anchor Press).

Thomas Midgley: taken from *http://listverse.com/science/10-inventors-killed-by-their-inventions/*.

"Yet according to this hypothesis": Samuel Taylor Coleridge, *Biographia Literaria*, ed. James Engell and Walter Jackson Bate (Princeton U. Press, 1983), 118-19.

Michael White on "pseudo-encopresis": Michael White, "The externalizing of the problem and the re-authoring of lives and relationships" in *Selected Papers* (Adelaide, Australia: Dulwich Centre Publications, 1988/89), 5-28, and "Pseudo-encopresis: From avalanche to victory, from vicious to virtuous cycles" also in *Selected Papers*, 115-124. White first published this work in 1984, in *Family Systems Medicine*, 2(2). And thanks, by the way, to Alex's dad, Richard Chasin, for pointing me to all this.

"those who study the origins of modern science tell a similar story": Steven Shapin and Simon Schaffer, *Leviathan and the Air-Pump* (Princeton U. Press, 1989).

Paul Ekman, *Emotions Revealed* (Times Books, 2003), xvi.

"the prime unit is not the verb": Jorge Luis Borges, *Labyrinths*, ed. Donald A. Yates and James E. Irby (New Directions, 1988), 8-9.

Chapter Four: Beginning Again

"Chaos and Complexity Theory": an earlier version of this section was published in *The Routledge Companion to Literature and Science*, ed. Bruce Clarke with Manuela Rossini

(Routledge, 2011), 41-50.

"I would not give a fig": Oliver Wendell Holmes (attributed).

"i accept chaos": Bob Dylan, liner notes to *Bringing It All Back Home* (record, Columbia Records, 1965).

"acute conversion experiences": see Ira Livingston, *Between Science and Literature: An Introduction to Autopoetics* (Illinois U. Press, 2006), 21-22, 85-89.

"Luhmann describes society as a complex system": Niklas Luhmann, *Political Theory in the Welfare State,* trans. J. Bednarz, Jr., (Berlin: de Gruyter, 1990), 83.

"his hair was a ragged mane": James Gleick, *Chaos: Making a New Science* (New York: Penguin, 1987), 2.

"Danger makes human beings intelligent": Anna Freud, *The Ego and the Mechanisms of Defence* (London: Hogarth Press, 1937).

"Chuang Tzu said": Chuang Tzu, *Basic Writings,* transl. Burton Watson (New York: Columbia University Press, 1964), 110.

"if what we are interested in is complexity itself": Ira Livingston, "Complex visuality: the radical middleground," in *Emergence and Embodiment: New Essays in Second-Order Systems Theory,* ed. Bruce Clarke and Mark Hansen (Durham, NC: Duke University Press, 2009) 246-262; 253.

"an observer's inability to define": William Rasch, *Niklas Luhmann's Modernity,* (Stanford, CA: Stanford University Press, 2000), 47.

"the contradiction between transcendence and embeddedness": see Ira Livingston, *Arrow of Chaos: Romanticism and Postmodernity* (Minneapolis: University of Minnesota Press, 1996) 84-104.

"In everyday language": Stephen Wolfram, *A New Kind of Science* (Champaign, Illinois: Wolfram Media, Inc., 2001), 557.

"Wolfram posits first 'that all processes'": *A New Kind of Science,* 715-717.

"crystallized from nothingness" (and subsequent quote): A. Gefter, "Something from nothing," review of F. Wilczek's *The*

Lightness of Being, in *New Scientist*, vol 199, No 2674, 9/20/08, 44.

"I call it *someness*": Judith Halberstam and Ira Livingston, eds.; *Posthuman Bodies* (Bloomington, Indiana: Indiana University Press, 1995), 8-9, or for a sustained account of Deleuze's concept of multiplicity, see Manuel de Landa's *Intensive Science and Virtual Philosophy* (London: Continuum, 2002).

"recursion in linguistics" (and subsequent quote): D. L. Everett, *Don't Sleep, There Are Snakes: Life and Language in the Amazonian Jungle* (New York: Pantheon, 2008), 240.

"Ian Hacking describes the process": in "Making Up People," in *London Review of Books* Vol. 28, No. 16: Aug. 17, 2006.

"Andrew Abbott's *Chaos of Disciplines*": (Chicago: University of Chicago Press, 2001).

"Jakobson defined *poeticity*": Roman Jakobson, "Linguistics and poetics," in *Style and Language*, ed. T. Sebeok (Cambridge, Mass.: MIT Press), 350-77.

"Alice Walker's . . .short story 'Everyday Use'": in *"Everyday Use" by Alice Walker* (Women Writers: Texts and Contexts), ed. B. Christian (New Jersey: Rutgers University Press).

"these hallucinations reflect": Oliver Sacks, "Patterns," in *The New York Times*, 2/13/08.

"what I have also called *withness*": Ira Livingston, *Between Science and Literature: An Introduction to Autopoetics* (Illinois U. Press, 2006), 4.

"merely a manifestation of a language": Michel Foucault, *The Order of Things*, (New York: Vintage, 1973), 300.

"In particular, I am not arguing that the science of chaos": N. Katherine Hayles, ed., *Chaos and Order: Complex Dynamics in Literature and Science* (Chicago: U of Chicago Press, 1991), 7.

"the 'topology' of a song" and subsequent quotes: David Owen, "The Soundtrack of Your Life," *New Yorker* 4/10/06, 66-71.

"a *New York Times* article surveying current scientific approaches to music": in Science Times section, 9/16/03; F4.

"humans are not alone in our musicality": Christine Kennedy, "Natural Rhythm," *New Scientist*, V. 197, No. 2644 (Feb. 23-29, 2008), 29-32, citing Cator, Hoy et al, in *Science* online, and Ava Chase in *Animal Learning and Behavior*, v. 29, p. 336.

"Everybody needs a bosom for a pillow": Cornershop, "Brimful of Asha," by Tijinder Singh, on *When I Was Born for the 7th Time* (record album, Wiiija/Luaka Bop/Warner Bros., 1997).

"Poetics and Autopoietics": This section comes out of discussions with my colleague Tracie Morris. I am grateful to her for particular points that helped shape this essay — for example, regarding the necessity of putting Heidegger's work into dialogue — in particular, with the work of J. L. Austin — but more than this, for all I continue to learn from her about poetics. And thanks to my old teacher Harley Henry, who spurred me on to study Romanticism. As I understand it, Harley also inspired his childhood friend Tommy Thompson to study philosophy. Thompson eventually left graduate school to become one of the original Red Clay Ramblers, whose classic rendition of "C-H-I-C-K-E-N" was my intro-duction to the song. I'm always happy to preach to the choir — in this case, the ones who already know that music is philosophy by other means — and vice versa — so thanks also to the choir for preaching to me.

"language, by naming beings for the first time": Martin Heidegger, *Poetry, Language, and Thought* (Harper, 2001), 71.

"the material is all the better": *Poetry, Language, and Thought*; 45-6.

"the more handy a piece of equipment is": *Poetry, Language, and Thought*; 63.

"in setting up a world": *Poetry, Language, and Thought*; 45-6.

"some particular entity": *Poetry, Language, and Thought*; 35.

"there is a crack in everything": Leonard Cohen, "Anthem," on *The Future* (record album, Sony, 1992).

"as self-opening cannot endure": *Poetry, Language, and Thought*;

47.

"upwardly mobile (evolving) biological life": Ira Livingston, *Between Science and Literature: An Introduction to Autopoetics* (Illinois U. Press, 2006), 135-136.

"C-H-I-C-K-E-N": of the many versions, I recommend Michelle Shocked on the original issue of *Arkansas Traveler* (record album, Polygram, 1992).

"in every era the attempt must be made anew": Walter Benjamin, "Theses on the Philosophy of History," in *Illuminations*, ed./intro. Hannah Arendt, transl. Harry Zohn (Harcourt Brace Jovanvich/Schocken, 1969), 253-264; 255.

"this unmediated character of a beginning": *Poetry, Language, and Thought*; 73.

"*lose* yourself in the music": Eminem (Marshall Mathers), "Lose Yourself," from *Eight Mile* (CD soundtrack from the film, various artists, Shady Records/Interscope Records, 2002).

"the destruction of every voice": Roland Barthes, *Image-Music-Text*, transl. Stephen Heath (Hill and Wang, 1978), 142.

Chapter Five: Ending and Returning

"If we go on in this way": Chuang Tzu, *Basic Writings*; transl. Burton Watson (New York: Columbia U. Press, 1964), 39.

"The poem of the mind in the act of finding": Wallace Stevens, "Of Modern Poetry," in *The Palm at the End of the Mind: Selected Poems*, ed. Holy Stevens (Random House/Vintage, 1972), 174-5.

"All imaginative and creative acts": Northrop Frye, *Fearful Symmetry: A Study of William Blake* (Princeton, New Jersey: Princeton University Press, 1972), 91.

"who threw their watches off the roof": Allen Ginsberg, *Howl and Other Poems* (City Lights Books, 1956).

Thomas Kuhn on "normal science": in *The Structure of Scientific Revolutions* (Third Ed., U. of Chicago Press, 1996).

"To get around this problem": Rachel Courtland, "Countdown to

Oblivion," in *New Scientist*, 10/2/2010, 6-7.

"While she poured him another glass of tea": Vladimir Nabokov, "Symbols and Signs," in *New Yorker*, May 15, 1948.

"Wind and helmsman held us on our course": from Homer, *The Odyssey*, transl. Ian Johnston (Richer Resources Publications; 2nd ed., 2006), Book Nine, lines 103-106.

"Visions! omens! hallucinations!": Allen Ginsberg, *Howl and Other Poems* (City Lights Books, 1956).

"Mona Lisa must have had the highway blues": Bob Dylan, "Visions of Johanna," *Blonde on Blonde* (record album, Columbia Records, 1966).

"There is a smile of love": William Blake, in *The Complete Poetry and Prose*, new rev. ed., ed. David Erdman (Garden City, N.Y.: Doubleday, Anchor Press).

zero
books

Contemporary culture has eliminated both the concept of the public and the figure of the intellectual. Former public spaces – both physical and cultural – are now either derelict or colonized by advertising. A cretinous anti-intellectualism presides, cheerled by expensively educated hacks in the pay of multinational corporations who reassure their bored readers that there is no need to rouse themselves from their interpassive stupor. The informal censorship internalized and propagated by the cultural workers of late capitalism generates a banal conformity that the propaganda chiefs of Stalinism could only ever have dreamt of imposing. Zer0 Books knows that another kind of discourse – intellectual without being academic, popular without being populist – is not only possible: it is already flourishing, in the regions beyond the striplit malls of so-called mass media and the neurotically bureaucratic halls of the academy. Zer0 is committed to the idea of publishing as a making public of the intellectual. It is convinced that in the unthinking, blandly consensual culture in which we live, critical and engaged theoretical reflection is more important than ever before.